THE POETICAL WORKS OF
EDWARD ROWLAND SILL

𝕳ousehold 𝕰dition

WITH ILLUSTRATIONS

BOSTON AND NEW YORK
HOUGHTON, MIFFLIN AND COMPANY
𝕮he 𝕽iverside 𝕻ress, 𝕮ambridge

PUBLISHERS' NOTE

THE first attempt to gather Mr. Sill's poems into a single volume was made in 1902, when Messrs. Houghton, Mifflin and Company issued a limited edition, combining the three small volumes previously published by them, and adding a few pieces never before collected. The compiler of that edition, Mr. William Belmont Parker, has also edited the present *Household Edition*, and has here arranged all the poems as nearly as possible in their chronological order. This new and more satisfactory grouping has prevented his making full use of the group titles that have become familiar to Mr. Sill's readers, but he has retained them as far as the conditions permit. The kind coöperation of Mrs. Sill, and of other surviving friends of the poet, has also made it possible to enlarge the collection materially, so that it contains all of his poetical writings that it is thought desirable to preserve.

BOSTON, September, 1906.

CONTENTS

THE HERMITAGE, AND OTHER POEMS

POEMS WRITTEN BETWEEN 1867 AND 1872

CONTENTS

CONTENTS

CONTENTS

CONTENTS

LIST OF ILLUSTRATIONS

BIOGRAPHICAL SKETCH

EDWARD ROWLAND SILL was born at Windsor, Connecticut, April 29, 1841, and died at Cleveland, Ohio, February 27, 1887. The forty-six years of his life furnish a record of quiet, modest service, unbroken by striking incident or conspicuous action. Teaching was his profession, though he did not at once adopt it. There was a period after his graduation from Yale, in 1861, when he was quite uncertain of his life work. He spent some years in California at various forms of business. Then, for a time, he attended the Divinity School at Harvard. Later, for a year, he tried the experiment of writing for a living. But in 1868 he determined upon teaching, and gave to it the best of his remaining years. He began characteristically at the bottom, taking a district school at Wadsworth, Ohio, later teaching at Cuyahoga Falls and at Oakland, California, and in 1874 he accepted the chair of English Literature at the University of California, where he taught until failing health put an end to his teaching, in 1882. He was happily married in 1867 to his cousin, Elizabeth Sill, who survives him. They had no children, which, perhaps, left him more completely free to devote himself, as he was fond of doing, to his students, who treasure his memory with an unusual and tender regard.

From his undergraduate years he had been writing, chiefly in verse, and contributing in a casual way to various periodicals, but keeping his authorship rigorously subordinate to his teaching. He was accustomed to say that he was " a teacher who occasionally wrote verses," and there was no affectation in his modesty; for he seldom cared to sign his poems, but sent them out either unsigned or signed only by a *nom de plume*. Gradually, however, his work began to gain recognition and increasing attention. It had been done so quietly that few realized how considerable in amount it was. In fact it was not until after his death that anything like an appraisal could be made of it, and most of his readers will probably be surprised to find his work so extensive as is indicated by this volume.

The body of Sill's work has three stages — the first marked by the angry rhetoric and unrestrained melody of his " Class Poem," the piece entitled " Music," and the poem of his first California period, " Summer Afternoon," with its soft assonances which suggest the influence of Mrs. Browning. The work of this period is worth reading chiefly as showing the course of Sill's development. To it belong practically the whole of the first volume, " The Hermitage and Other Poems," published in 1868.

The second period covers the years from 1867 to

1880, including almost all the years of his teaching service. The poems of this period seem to have lost the sensuousness of the earlier time, and not yet to have gained the clear tone and firm texture of the later period. They are more subjective, more austere, and at times suggest the schoolmaster. Some are frankly pedagogic in tone and substance, as " The Schoolhouse Windows," " The Clocks of Gnoster-Town," and " Berkeley Greets New Haven." Among them are the keenest poems of irony, " Fantasy and First Love," " The Tree of my Life " and " Five Lives." To this period belong also two or three of the strongest poems of ethical impulse that he wrote. The best known of all his poems, " The Fool's Prayer," of which Professor Royce has made such impressive use in the concluding chapter of " The Spirit of Modern Philosophy," was first published in " The Atlantic Monthly " for April, 1879, and the other poem which is so often coupled with it, " Opportunity," appeared in " The Californian " in November, 1880.

" Five Lives " and " The Fool's Prayer " are the two poems which, perhaps, best sum up the two tendencies of Sill's mind during the middle period, the time of crystallization of his philosophy of life. They show his keen sense of unwelcome truth, on the biological and the moral side; his courageous acceptance of it and his scornful rejection of subterfuges, which he put forcibly in " Truth at Last."

The third and closing period of Sill's work was all too short. It began with his return from California to Ohio, in 1883, and ended with his most regrettable death, in 1887. It was a period of rapid maturing, both in thought and craftsmanship. He did not enter new fields. He had no new message, but he gave the old message without uncertainty or wavering or confusion. Now that it came clear and plain the message was perceived to be Emersonian, Arnoldian, if you please, Tennysonian, perhaps. At any rate all three strains were in the music. But it was sung by a new voice, — a voice that gained steadily in flexibility, in timbre, and in tone. Now for the first time the singer learned to use its full range. For the first time he ventured into humor and delicate irony and graceful raillery. To this period belong " Momentous Words," " The Agile Sonneteer," " The Poet's Political Economy," and " A Subtlety," all tinged with irony, to be sure, but all lighted with genuine humor. As he went on he touched the life-long themes more firmly and more confidently. His message was always ethical : work, fear not, trust God, hope evermore and believe ; but it gained in grace and persuasiveness. There remained an undertone of wistfulness, but it was merged in confident faith, so that " A Second Thought," — which seems to have been the last poem he wrote — faces the future with a front as brave as Browning's " Prospice."

Most of his poems were not published in book form

until after his death, but two volumes appeared in his lifetime. " The Hermitage and Other Poems" was published by Leypoldt and Holt in 1868, and " The Venus of Milo and Other Poems" was privately printed at Berkeley, California, in 1883. Following his death there were published by Houghton, Mifflin and Company " Poems " in 1887, " The Hermitage and Later Poems " in 1889, and " Hermione and Other Poems " in 1900. In 1900 there also appeared under the imprint of Houghton, Mifflin and Company a volume of prose selections taken chiefly from his contributions to the " Atlantic," and entitled " The Prose of Edward Rowland Sill." No life of Sill has yet been published, though the Memorial Volume privately printed at Berkeley, California, contains an account of his life, accompanied by a number of his letters.

UNDERGRADUATE AND
EARLY POEMS

THE POLAR SEA

At the North, far away,
Rolls a great sea for aye,
Silently, awfully.
Round it on every hand
Ice-towers majestic stand,
Guarding this silent sea
Grimly, invincibly.
Never there man hath been,
Who hath come back again,
Telling to ears of men
What is this sea within.
Under the starlight,
Rippling the moonlight,
Drinking the sunlight,
Desolate, never heard nor seen,
Beating forever it hath been.

From our life far away
Roll the dark waves, for aye,

Of an Eternity,
Silently, awfully.
Round it on every hand
Death's icy barriers stand,
Guarding this silent sea
Grimly, invincibly.
Never there man hath been
Who could return again,
Telling to mortal ken
What is within the sea
Of that Eternity.

Terrible is our life —
In its whole blood-written history
Only a feverish strife;
In its beginning, a mystery —
In its wild ending, an agony.
Terrible is our death —
Black-hanging cloud over Life's setting sun,
Darkness of night when the daylight is done.
In the shadow of that cloud,
Deep within that darkness' shroud,
Rolls the ever-throbbing sea;
And we — all we —
Are drifting rapidly
And floating silently
Into that unknown sea —
Into Eternity.

MORNING

I ENTERED once, at break of day,
A chapel, lichen-stained and gray,
Where a congregation dozed and heard
An old monk read from a written Word.
No light through the window-panes could pass,
For shutters were closed on the rich stained-glass;
And in a gloom like the nether night
The monk read on by a taper's light.
Ghostly with shadows, that shrank and grew
As the dim light flared, were aisle and pew;
And the congregation that dozed around
Listened without a stir or sound —
Save one, who rose with wistful face,
And shifted a shutter from its place.
Then light flashed in like a flashing gem —
For dawn had come unknown to them —
And a slender beam, like a lance of gold,
Shot to the crimson curtain-fold,
Over the bended head of him
Who pored and pored by the taper dim;
And it kindled over his wrinkled brow
Such words: "The law which was till now;"
And I wondered that, under that morning ray,
When night and shadow were scattered away,

MORNING

The monk should bow his locks of white
By a taper's feebly flickering light —
Should pore, and pore, and never seem
To notice the golden morning-beam.

MIDNIGHT [1]

Under the stars, across whose patient eyes
The wind is brushing flecks of filmy cloud,
I wait for kindly night to hush and calm
The wrangling throng of cares and discontents,
The tangled troubles of a feverish brain.
From far-off church-towers, distance-muffled bells
Are slowly tolling dying midnight's age.
A surging wind sighs through the shadowy trees,
Like surf that breaks on an invisible beach,
And sends a spray of whispers on the air.
I hear the rushing of the wings of Time
Sweep by me. Voices of the murmuring Past
Chant a low dirge above my kneeling heart.
I hear — or is it only the wild wind
Telling its ghostly dreams to the dark trees? —
Amid its pauses, as irresolute
And purposeless it gropes in fitful gusts
Throughout the darkness, sounds of years ago.
Sometimes it seems the rustle of a step,
Which made my heart beat in those years ago —
Which makes me weep to listen for it now;

---

[1] The editor has retained this poem as illustrating Sill's early manner, in
spite of the fact that several lines from it reappear unchanged in later
poems; see pp. 95, 125, 126.

Sometimes a little foolish whispered phrase,
That you would smile at, if one uttered it —
At which I smiled even as I treasured it;
A warm breath brushing lightly by my cheek —
A low-toned fragment of a sad old song —
I almost think them real, so crazed am I,
Till the shrill wind whirls them in scorn away,
And shrieks its laughter far into the gloom.
Oh, brooding night! thou mockest so bitterly
With thy wild visions and thy weird-winged wind,
That I could well believe thee all unreal,
And our whole world only a phantasy,
And we far-slanted shadows of some life
That walks between our planet and its God.
Oh, stars of Heaven! will ye not comfort me?
Voices of brother-men from long ago,
Come up to me, clasped in the leaves of books,
That tell how they too dreamed the dream of life,
And how, over Earth's flitting phantom forms
Ye shone serene and steadfast as to-night.
Unseal, unseal the secret, for whose hour
Ye wait in hushed and breathless watchfulness
Till God reveal the mystery of His will.
Is it not time to tell us why we live?
So many years we sleep, and wake, and sleep,
While — like some Magian through the mysteries
Leading in fear the blindfold neophyte —
Time leads us dimly on, till angrily
Tired life would turn and throttle its stern guide,

Till he should tell us *whither* and *how long*.
But Time gives back no answer, and the stars
Burn on, cold, hushed, and changeless as before,
And we go back baffled and stolidly
To the old, weary, hollow-hearted world;
To the old, endless search for life in death —
The restless, hopeless roaming after rest.

FAITH

THE tree-top, high above the barren field,
    Rising beyond the night's gray folds of mist,
Rests stirless where the upper air is sealed
    To perfect silence, by the faint moon kiss'd.
But the low branches, drooping to the ground,
    Sway to and fro, as sways funereal plume,
While from their restless depths low whispers sound:
    " We fear, we fear the darkness and the gloom ;
    Dim forms beneath us pass and reappear,
    And mournful tongues are menacing us here."

Then from the topmost bough falls calm reply :
    " Hush, hush !   I see the coming of the morn ;
Swiftly the silent Night is passing by,
    And in her bosom rosy Dawn is borne.
    'T is but your own dim shadows that ye see,
    'T is but your own low moans that trouble ye."

So Life stands, with a twilight world around ;
Faith turned serenely to the steadfast sky,
Still answering the heart that sweeps the ground,
Sobbing in fear, and tossing restlessly —
    " Hush, hush ! The Dawn breaks o'er the Eastern
        sea,
    'T is but thine own dim shadow troubling thee."

MUSIC

The little rim of moon hangs low — the room
Is saintly with the presence of Night,
And Silence broods with knitted brows around.
The woven lilies of the velvet floor
Blend with the roses in the dusky light,
Which shows twin pictures glimmering from the walls:
Here, a mailed group kneels by the rocky sea —
There, a gray desert, and a well, and palms ;
While the faint perfume of a violet,
Vague as a dream of Spring, pervades the air.
Where the moon gleams along the organ-front,
The crooked shadow of a dead branch stirs
Like ghostly fingers gliding through a tune.
Now rises one with faintly rustling robes,
And white hands search among the glistening keys.
Out of the silence sounds are forming — tones
That seem to come from infinite distances, —
Soft trebles fluttering down like snowy doves
Just dipping their swift wings in the deep bass
That crumbles downward like a crumbling wave ;
And out of those low-gathering harmonies
A voice arises, tangled in their maze,
Then soaring up exultantly alone,
While the accompaniment wails and complains.

— I am upon the seashore. 'T is the sound
Of ocean, surging on against the land.
That throbbing thunder is the roar of surf
Beaten and broken on the frothy rocks.
Those whispering trebles are the plashing waves
That ripple up the smooth sand's slope, and kiss
The tinkling shells with coy lips, quick withdrawn;
And over all, the solitary voice
Is the wind wandering on its endless quest.
— A change comes, in a crash of minor chords.
I am a dreamer, waking from his dream
Into the life to which our life is sleep.
My soul is floating — floating, till afar
The round Earth rolls, with fleece of moonlit
      cloud,
A globe of amber, gleaming as it goes.
Deep in some hollow cavern of the sky
All human life is pleading to its God.
Still the accompaniment wails and complains; —
A wild confusion of entangled chords,
Revenge, and fear, and strong men's agony,
The shrill cry of despair, the slow, deep swell
Of Time's long effort, sinking but to swell,
While woman's lonely love, and childhood's faith
Go wandering with soft whispers hand in hand.
Suddenly from the ages one pure soul
Is singled out to plead before the Throne;
And then again the solitary voice
Peals up among the stars from the great throng,

Catching from out the storm all love, all hope,
All loveliness of life, and utters it.

Then the hushed music sobs itself to sleep,
And all is still, — save the reluctant sigh
That tells the wakening from immortal dreams.

DREAM–DOOMED

A MAID upon the lonely beach,
  All in the silent, summer day,
  With wide blue eyes fixed far away,
And small hands clinging each to each.

All day she wanders by the sea; —
  What are the ways of men to her,
  Whose soul is busy with the stir
Of never-resting memory?

For there had glanced a passing gleam
  Of love all hopeless on her way,
  And life's up-springing April day
God's hand had darkened with a dream.

The mist floats on the desert's face,
  And lake and isle all lustrous moulds, —
  But when withdrawn its billowy folds,
How bare and desolate the place!

Why should she live? The life above
  Can scarce be sadder than her own;
  But shall she die? For death alone
Can still the fluttering wing of love.

When darkness on the ocean hangs,
   She hears the loud surf tumbling in,
   The loose stones jostling with a din
Like wild beast clashing-to his fangs.

Under the leaden morning sky,
   She sees from off the toppling comb
   The mad wind snatching flecks of foam
To whirl them wildly drifting by.

And when, as daylight disappears,
   The large moon upward moveth slow,
   It seems to waver, shrink, and grow,
Trembling through such a mist of tears.

But when the evening zephyrs blow
   A music borne from off the sea,
   She mingles with the melody
A plaintive song, all soft and low.

Calmly the night comes down on all the land,
   Faintly the twilight glimmers o'er the sea,
Sadly the lingering ripples kiss the sand,
   So sad I pace the beach and wait for thee.

Soft steal the muffled inland echoes here,
   A sound of church-bells trembles on the lea, —
So softly, muffled memories meet the ear,
   And seem to mock me as I wait for thee.

Solemnly still the great, calm stars glow on,
    And all the broad, fair heaven leans silently,
While slumberous Ocean's undulous undertone
    Still whispers with me as I wait for thee.

Upon the strand where life's loud surges beat,
    My footsteps follow where my hope must be;
The dull, long days and nights break at my feet —
    Must I forever, weeping, wait for thee?

———————

Low lowers the dull-eyed winter's day —
    A sullen sky the ocean mocks;
    The surf beats bitterly the rocks,
Which wintry years have worn away.

Chafing within its cragged cage,
    The wave again and still again
    Leaps fiercely up its length of chain,
To fall back foaming in its rage.

On the wet sands, with elfish hair,
    And faded fingers tightly clenched,
    And vest whose folds, all weather-drenched,
Leave half her haggard bosom bare,

She stands amid the spray, alone.
    O heavy heart! that all thy years
    Hast held one image dim with tears,
And watched it while it turned to stone.

So wretched stands she staring there,
  As if the desert and the storm
  And bitter wind had taken form,
And frozen into that despair.

And looking on them thus I seem
  To understand the life undone,
  The life-long wretchedness of one
Whose youth was withered with a dream.

DESPAIR AND HOPE

WE sailed a cruise on a summer sea —
I, and a skull for company :
I in the stern our course to turn,
And it on the prow to grin at me.
Over the deep heaven, hung below,
Whose imaged clouds lay white like snow,
Glided we, as the tide might be,
Slipping swiftly, floating slow.
Past the woods all living green —
Save by the marge some fading tree,
Whose leaf, so early autumn-touched,
Would make the skull to grin at me.

Past a grove of fragrant pine,
From whose dusky depths of shade
Snowy shaft and colonnade
Marked a ruined altar-shrine ; —
And the skull's grim face grinned into mine.
Under the arch of a vine-clasped elm
Leaning off from the mossy land,
Across the shallow the idle helm
Lightly furrowed the silver sand :
Down the slope all clover-sweet
Danced a group in childish glee —

Hissed a swift snake at their feet; —
    Then the skull grinned unto me.

Into a cavern dim and dank
    Crept we on the creeping tide;
Shapeless creatures rose and sank,
    Dripped with damp the ceiling wide.
Darker, chiller hung the air;
    Scarcely I the prow could see;
But I, through the shadow there,
    Felt the skull still grin at me.

Out of the cavern's thither side,
    Into a mellow, morn-like glow,
Streams the ripple-curving tide;
    Sounds of music sweeter grow;
Odorous incense, softened air,
Melodies so faint and fair,
    Thrill me through with life and love:
And all suddenly from the prow,
Where had seemed the skull just now,
    Flutters to my breast a dove.

COMMENCEMENT POEM

I

1

Four years!
Four waves of that wide sea which rings the world
Broken upon the shore, eternity.
Upon whose crests, like waifs tossed by the tide,
We neared, touched, floated side by side, and now
Sad is their murmur on the shadowy sand,
And sad our parting as we drift away.

2

Four years!
Fled like the phantoms of a morning dream —
A strange, fair dream, and now the sun has risen,
And the day's work begun.   Yet blame us not
If, while we gird ourselves, we linger still
Wistfully musing over what we dreamed.

II

O hours of Yale — vanished hours!
 Memory, sorrowfully singing,
 Makes a far-off sound, like ringing
  Of a chime of silver bells,
  Whose soft music sinks and swells,

Breathed upon by a breath of flowers;
Fainter, sweeter fragrance bringing
Than from odorous island-dells,
Kissed all night by summer showers.

III

1

Mornings were there, richer than of Eastern story,
When the dark, wet trunks the sun-bathed elms
uphold,
Bedded in the leaves whose lustrous glory
Half was sheen of emeralds, half of lucent gold.

2

Evenings when the sun set, like a king departed
Unto other lands with revel, pomp, and light,
While the queenly moon, deserted, pale, proud-hearted,
Paces the still corridors of the stars all night.

3

Hours of golden noonday, when the blood up-leaping
Like a soft, swift lightning pulses through the veins;
Hours of shrouded midnight, when the soul unsleeping
Calm self-knowledge, wider trust, and patience gains.

4

Friendships truer than all woman's brittle passion,
Love that in its fullness, even while we stand
Here, to part, has only stammering expression,
Dumb and half-embarrassed clinging hand to hand.

IV

1

Here at last to part — the darkness lying
  In that parting not as yet we know;
Like a child who sees his father dying,
  With a vague, half-wondering sense of woe.

2

As, when some Beloved has departed,
  In the after years, unfelt before,
Haunting wishes vex the heavy-hearted, —
  " Would to God that we had loved him more ! "

3

So we, o'er these buried years low-bending,
  Shall regret each lightest cause of pain,
Trivial hurts in silent heartaches ending,
  Till we sigh, " Would we might live again ! "

4

All our foolish pride and willful blindness,
  Darkening round us like a cloud of dust,
Careless scorn, where should have been all kindness,
  Cold suspicion in the place of trust,

5

Many a word we might have left unspoken,
  Many a deed that should have been undone,
Shall reproach us from each treasured token
  With a separate sting for every one.

6

When the world is heavy on our shoulders,
　　And the heart is fretted with its care, —
When the glory of ambition moulders,
　　And our load seems more than we can bear, —

7

When the days and nights, like shuttles weaving
　　In a senseless loom, pass to and fro,
Sombre hues in faded patterns leaving
　　On the woof of life that lies below,

8

Through the dim, long years old forms will glimmer,
　　Ghostly lips will haunt us with their tone,
Kind eyes will look forth, and seem the dimmer
　　For the memories brimming in their own.

9

We go forth, like children in the morning
　　Scattering to spend the summer hours, —
Some their brows with laurel wreaths adorning,
　　Some to saunter through a field of flowers ;

10

One to lose his way, and wander, straying,
　　Till the twilight, frighted and alone, —
One, it may be, weary with his playing,
　　Wending home his footsteps ere the noon.

II

But whatever fate to us is given,
　　All, when day is done, again shall meet,
And at night-fall, 'neath the stars of heaven,
　　Shall be gathered at our Father's feet.

V

RETROSPECT

Not all which we have been
　　Do we remain,
Nor on the dial-hearts of men
　　Do the years mark themselves in vain;
But every cloud that in our sky hath passed,
Some gloom or glory hath upon us cast;
And there have fallen from us, as we traveled,
　　Many a burden of an ancient pain —
Many a tangled cord hath been unraveled,
　　Never to bind our foolish hearts again.
Old loves have left us, lingeringly and slow,
As melts away the distant strain of low
Sweet music — waking us from troubled dreams,
Lulling to holier ones — that dies afar
On the deep night, as if by silver beams
Claspt to the trembling breast of some charmed star.
And we have stood and watched, all wistfully,
While fluttering hopes have died out of our lives,
As one who follows with a straining eye
A bird that far, far-off fades in the sky,

A little rocking speck — now lost — and still he
    strives
A moment to recover it — in vain,
Then slowly turns back to his work again.
But loves and hopes have left us in their place,
Thank God! a gentle grace,
A patience, a belief in His good time,
Worth more than all earth's joys to which we climb.

VI

The pleasant path of youth that we have ranged
    Ends here; as children we lie down this even,
    But while we sleep there is a stir in heaven —
A hundred guardian angels have been changed.
Those of our childhood gently have departed
    With its pure record, writ on lilies, sealed;
And in their place stand spirits sterner-hearted,
    To grave our manhood on a brazen shield.

VII

I

Well, the world is before us, — let us go forth and
    live,
    God's fair stars overhead, and the breath of God
      within,
    Steadfast as we may amid the whirl and the din;
Let us challenge the fates, — what answer do they
    give?

2

Work, work, work!
All action is noble and grand —
Whirling the wheel or tilling the land,
In the honest blows of the brawny hand
Is the kingliest crown of living won :
Work, work, work!

3

Ah! but the hollowness will lurk
Under the shell of all that is done.
Where is the labor so noble and great,
Among all vanities under the sun?
What is the grandeur of serving a state,
Whose tail is stinging its head to death like a scorpion?
To simper over a counter, to lie for a piece of coin,
To be shrewd and cunning, to cheat and steal,
Business-like and mercantile, —
An army of rats and foxes — who will join?
Each little busy brain forever at work
Webbing out its mite of a plan,
Each hypocritical face with smile and smirk,
Thinking to mask its spleen from another man :
And then the apish mummery
Of the thing they call Society!
And its poor, sour fools that smiling stand,
With a smile that is overdone, —
With a hand that graspeth each man's hand,
And a heart that loveth none.

And the mills and shops whose dull routine
Turns God's image to a machine:
Oh! it makes one proud of our civilization —
Proud of a place in the noble nation,
Where a human soul —
A human soul —
Passes the years as they onward roll,
Making a million of heads for pins, or a thousand
     knives;
Such are the miracles men call lives!

4

No wonder, when the future is forgot,
If earth, and man, and all that being brings,
Seem but a blank, unmeaning blot,
That God has scattered, writing higher things,
And the soul, poor ghost!
So bitterly, bitterly tempest-tost,
So base and cowardly doth lie,
That it would give —
Ah! gladly give —
All this life that it dare not live,
To shun the death it dare not die.
Life — poor thing — that wastes its painful breath,
And walks the road that the fates have given,
Tossing its fettered hands to heaven,
Like an ironed criminal struggling and praying his
     way to death!

5

DISCONTENT

Oh, that one could arise and flee
Unto blue-eyed Italy,
Far from mechanical clank and hum !
There to sit by the sighing sea,
And to dream of the days that shall be — shall be —
And the glory of years to come.
Or on some far ocean-isle,
Under the palm and the cocoa-tree,
To build of the coral boughs a home, —
Or floating and falling adown the Nile,
To drown one's cares in the deeps of Time
And the desert's brooding mystery.
Yet howsoever we plot or plan,
In every age — through every clime —
Still the littleness of man
Would follow us, fast as we might flee :
And the wrangling world break in on whatever is
        tender and sweet,
As on a beautiful tune the rattling and noise of the
        street.

6

Oh, the world — the world !
Mockery — knavery — cheat ;
Down at your angry feet
Let the lying thing be hurled :

Worth no sorrowful tear or sob,
Worth not even a sigh;
But the scorn which a murdered purpose hurls on a
      butchering mob, —
Which the pale, dead lips of a truth smile back on a
      conquering lie.

VIII

THE FOUNTAIN

   Were it not horrible?
After all the dreams we dream,
   Our yearnings and our prayers,
If this " I " were but a stream
Of thoughts, sensations, joys, and pains,
Which being clogged, no soul remains;
Even as the fountain seems to be
A shape of one identity,
But only is a stream of drops,
And when the swift succession stops,
The fountain melts and disappears,
Leaving no trace but scattered tears.
Yet even here, O foolish heart,
Thou wert not cheated of thy part;
Were it not better, even here,
To keep thy current pure and clear,
With pearly drops of dew to wet
The amaranth and violet,

And round thy crystal feet to shower
Blessings and beauty every hour—
Better than in a sullen flow
To creep along the ground, and go
Wasting and sinking through the sand,
To make no single spot of land
Happier or holier for thy being —
Refresh no flower, no grass-blade, seeing
Thou wert not always thus to stand?

IX

SOLITUDE

All alone — alone,
Calm, as on a kingly throne,
Take thy place in the crowded land,
Self-centred in free self-command.
Let thy manhood leave behind
The narrow ways of the lesser mind:
What to thee are its little cares,
The feeble love or the spite it bears?
Let the noisy crowd go by —
In thy lonely watch on high,
Far from the chattering tongues of men,
Sitting above their call or ken,
Free from links of manner and form
Thou shalt learn of the winged storm —
God shall speak to thee out of the sky.

X

Well — well,
Why need the hurrying brain to trouble itself?
Threescore years is swiftly worn away —
In some summer when our heads are gray,
We perhaps shall wander back from our power or
     pelf,
To muse on the days when all these things befell.
Nothing will then be changed:
Calm as of yore through the slumberous summer
     noon
Will the Old Rock rest in its majesty;
All the paths that we have ranged
Still will wear the glory of their June, —
Nothing changed but we.
The years will bring us, hastening to their goal,
A little more of calmness, and of trust,
With still the old, old doubt of death and dust,
And still the expectancy within the soul.
O Father, as we go to meet the years,
We ask not joy that fame or pleasure brings,
But some calm knowledge of the sum of things —
A hint of glory glimmering over tears;
That he, who walks with sanction from Thy hand,
Some token of its presence may have seen,
Beneath which we may tread the path serene
Into the stillness of the unknown land.

THE FOUR PICTURES

A GROUP of artists of the olden time
Met in a studio. One was gray and bent,
With beard like snow against his doublet black;
Three younger, one with glowing olive cheek,
One with a drowsy glitter in deep eyes,
One lean, and full of quick heat-lightning ways, —
You could not guess if he were old or young,
For his face hid the marks of other lives
Long gone, and so belied his stripling form.

Around were half-done pictures: eyes begun,
Gleams of white flesh from sombre shadows dim,
A velvet mantle tossed upon a stool,
A lute, a leaning rapier, vases tall,
And thro' thin, taper glasses glimmered wine.

Suddenly spake the restless one: " Enough
Of dabbled flowers, and bits of landscape bland;
Let us each paint the world as 't is to him.
Here are my pencils and my canvas, — come! "
Then from a curious cabinet he drew
A flask, vine-etched, and held it to the sun,
Till the gold was molten thro' it: " This to him
Whose sketch is best — but who shall be the judge? "

" That sweet slim maid who sat to you last week,"
Answered the graybeard, " and who comes to-day,
You said, with ducats for the finished work."

So till the sunset's level pencil lay
Flame red on bust and antique furniture,
Their slender fingers dextrous went and came
'Twixt color and canvas; then they turned and saw.

Snowbeard had sketched a sullen close of day;
A flat and windy beach; a flying leaf
Whirled at haphazard over toward the foam.

And Drowsy-eyes had hung a pipe in air,
Broken mid-stem, whose tip was lost in cloud,
And from its bowl a bubble floated up,
Which was the earth, with land and mimic seas.

And Olive-cheek had made far overhead
A gorge of blue in the sky, with cliffs of cloud
Rounded, and white as salt, and in between
A headlong fallen angel plunging down.

But Restless-face most lovingly had drawn
The slim sweet maid who was to be their judge,
Looking with such unearthly deeps of eyes
Into your very soul, you dare not love —
You dare not even dream how fair they were,
Lest they should flash upon your dream with scorn.

And as they looked, lo! she herself had come.
Quietly then the others stole away,
With friendly mischief in their nod and smile,
Leaving those two alone. From silken mesh
She drew the broad gold pieces, that betrayed
Her trembling touch in tinklings musical.
But he: " I give you all the world I have, —
I ask but what is all the world to me."
And answering not, with tender eyes cast down,
She left in his her little, warm, white hand.

HOUSE WHERE SILL WAS BORN, WINDSOR, CONN., 1841

POEMS WRITTEN BETWEEN
1862 AND 1867

THE RUBY HEART

A CHILD'S STORY

UNDER a fragrant blossom-bell
A tiny Fairy once did dwell.
The moss was bright about her feet,
Her little face was fair and sweet,
Her form in rainbow hues was clad,
And yet the Fairy's soul was sad ;
For, of the Elves that round her moved,
And in the yellow moonlight roved,
There was no Spirit that she loved.

Many a one there was, I ween,
Among the sprites that danced the green,
Whose hands were warm to clasp her own,
And voices kindly in their tone ;
But love the fondest and the best
Awaked no answer in her breast :
Her heart unmoved within her slept —
And, " I can never love ! " she wept.

She taught herself a quaint old song
And crooned it over all day long:

"*He prayeth best, who loveth best*
All things both great and small;
For the dear God who loveth us,
He made and loveth all."

"But I," she said, "can never pray,
Nor to His mansions find the way,
For he will suffer not, I know,
A creature unto Him to go
Who has not loved His world below."

Slow-wandering by the brook alone,
She chose a pure white pebble-stone,
And carved it, sitting there apart,
Into a little marble heart;
She hung it by her mossy bed —
"My heart will never love," she said,
"Till this white stone turn ruby-red."

One night a moonbeam smote her face
And wakened her, and in its place
There stood an angel, full of grace.
"Dear child," he said, "from far above
I come to teach thee how to love.
Do every day some little deed
Of kindness, some faint creature feed,

Make some hurt spirit cease to bleed,
Then carve the record fair, at night,
Upon thy heart of marble white.
Each word shall turn to ruby-red,
And so much of thy task be sped; —
For when the whole is ruddied o'er,
Thy bosom shall be cold no more;
The souls thy careless thoughts contemn
Shall win thee by *thy* deeds to *them*."

Upon the sorrowful Fairy broke
Like sudden sunshine this new hope.
Each day to some one's door she took
A kindly act, or word, or look,
Whose record, fairly carved at night,
Blushed out upon the stony white;
Till, somehow, wondrously there grew
More grace in every one she knew —
Each little ugliness concealed,
Each goodness more and more revealed, —
As, when you watch the twilight through,
The sky seems one pure empty blue,
Till, o'er the paling sunset bars,
Suddenly 't is one sweep of stars!

So day by day she found herself
Grow kindlier to each little elf:
Yea, even to the birds and bees,
And slender flowerets round her knees;

The very moss-buds at her feet
She came with warmer smile to greet,
Till now, at last, her marble heart
Was ruddy, save one little part
That gleamed all snowy as of old
In the still moonbeams, white and cold.

Her task was almost done — she knelt,
And hid her glad wet eyes, and felt
Her soul's first prayer steal up to God,
Like Spring's first violet from the sod.
Through all her being softly stole
Such joy of gratitude, her soul
Brimmed over like a brimming cup —
And then a voice said, " Child, look up ! "
And lo ! the stone above her head
Was a pure ruby, starry-red ;
And down among the flowers there flew,
Brushing aside the moonlit dew,
A little snowy elfin dove,
And nestled on her breast, to prove
Sweet trust in one whose heart was love.

TO CHILD ANNA

As in the Spring, ere any flowers have come,
  A vague and blossomy smell
Pervades the woods, all odors mixed in one,
      As if to tell
  That they are mustering in each sunny dell,

So round your childish form there seems to cling
  A sense of nameless grace,
A sweet confusion — budding hints of Spring
      Just giving place
  To graver woman-shadows in your face.

I see no longer the mere child you are —
  The woman you might be
Stands in your place, with eyes that gaze afar :
      Her face I see,
  And it is very beautiful to me.

The little soft white hands you lay in mine
  I touch with reverent care ;
I see them wrinkled into many a line,
      But fair — more fair
  For every weary deed they do and bear.

The fresh young mouth, all careless purity,
   Has faded from my gaze,
And all the tender looks, which charity
        And many patient days
   Leave round the lips, seem now to take its place.

Therefore I stroke so tenderly your head,
   Or watch your steps afar,
Praying that God His love on you will shed —
        More faithful far
   Than our blind human love and watching are.

A FABLE

TO CHILD ANNA

ONE morning, in a Prince's park,
Before the rising of the lark
Or the first glimmering twilight beam,
A Lily blossomed by a stream;
Just at the chillest, darkest hour,
When frowning clouds in heaven lower,
When shadows crouch all gaunt and grim,
And every little star is dim.
  " O dreary world!" the Lily sighed:
Only the dreary wind replied.
  Soon, in the East uprising slow,
A cold gray dawn began to grow.
The Lily watched where all around
The mist came creeping o'er the ground,
And listened, while with sadder tone
The morning-wind began to moan:
But all the more the light drew on,
Her tear-dewed cheek was deathlier wan, —
Each streak of daylight, as it grew,
Revealed a world so strange and new.
Slowly the dawn crept up the sky
Like a cold, cruel, watching eye.

Once from some little wakened bird
A twittering note of joy she heard :
The chill dew fell upon her head —
She almost wished that she were dead ;
"There comes no joy for me," she said.

    A gnarled and wisdom-wrinkled Oak
Which overheard, in answer spoke :
    "O foolish little Lilybell,
Why do you weep, when all is well ?
Look up ! Have faith ! For by and by
The sun is coming up the sky ;
All golden red the heavens will glow,
All golden green the earth below ;
The birds their rippling songs will sing,
And wooing winds their spices bring :
And then the Prince will hither come
To wander 'mid his flowers, and some
(Ah, favored blossoms !), bending down,
He plucks and places in his crown.
Look up, O foolish Lilybell !
A little while, and all is well."

    The Lily drooped and trembled still :
"The dawn," she sobbed, "is dim and chill ;
And if the Prince should come, alas !
He will not stoop among the grass ;
I surely cannot please his eyes,
For I am neither fair nor wise :
He 'll choose some tall and stately tree,
He surely will not care for me ! "

But now the sunrise was at hand,
Lighting with splendor all the land;
As if a seraph stood below
With lifted pinions all aglow,
Whose tips of fire still nearer came
In feathery plumes of floating flame;
While from his hidden face the rays
Shot up and set the heavens ablaze.
They warmed the old Oak's wrinkled face,
And touched it with a mellow grace;
Then dancing downward to his feet
They kissed the Lily's face so sweet,
And laughed away her foolish fear
And lit a gem in every tear;
Then flew to greet the Master's eye,
Who even now was drawing nigh.

He saw the Lily's fragile cup
With dew and sunlight brimming up,
And, as he marked each beauty well,
The petals pure as pearliest shell,
And on the lowly bending stem
The tear-drop sparkling like a gem,
The Prince was glad, and stooping down
Plucked it, and set it in his crown;
And 'mid the jewels glittering there
None shone so royally and rare,
For none was half so pure and fair.

Dear child, 't is our ingratitude,
And faithless fear, and sullen mood,

Darken a world so bright and good!
There 's nothing beautiful and true —
There 's not a rift of heaven's blue,
And not a flower, or dancing leaf,
But shames our selfish-hearted grief.
His hand that feels the sparrow's fall,
And builds the bee his castle-wall,
And spreads the tiniest insect's sail,
And tints the violet's purple veil,
Will never let His children stray
Or wander from His arms away.
To-day may seem all cold and dim —
Trust the To-morrow unto Him.

   'T is slander that we often hear,
" Hope whispers falsehoods in our ear," —
There 's no such lying voice as Fear.
Hope is a prophet sent from Heaven,
Fear is a false and croaking raven.
The dawn that buds all gray and cold
Will blossom to a sky of gold ;
God's love shall like a sunrise stay
To lighten all the future way —
Still brighter to the Perfect Day.

THE CREATION

A Fountain rusheth upward from God's throne;
Its streaming stem we name Eternal Power:
Its tossing drops are worlds, that spin and fall,
While on their spheres our little human lives
Like gleams and shadows swiftly glance and go.

THE FIRST CAUSE

DOUBTLESS the linnet, shut within its cage,
Thinks the fair child that loves it, brings it seed,
And hangs it, chirping to it, in the sun,
Is the preserver of its little world.

Doubtless the child, within her nursery walls,
Thinks her kind father is the father of all
Those happy children, chattering on the lawn —
Keeps yonder town as well as this bright room,
And pours the brook that sparkles past the door.

Doubtless we think the Being who made man,
The visible world, space powdered thick with stars,
The golden fruit whose core is curious life,
Created all things — love, and law, and death;
Fate, the crowned forehead; Will, the sceptred hand.

Perchance — perchance: yet need it be that He
Who planted us is the Head-gardener? What
If beyond Him rose rank on rank, as the bulb
Is higher than the crystals of its food,
And he who sets it, higher than the flower,
And he that owns the garden, more than all?

The great Cause works through lesser ones; permits
The plant to bear dead buds on dying stems;
The beaver to weave dams that the stream snaps;
The workman to make watches that lose time,

Or organ pipes all jarred and out of tune.
Did not I build a playhouse for my boys,
And made it ill, and that loose plank fell down
And hurt the children ? And did not I learn,
After three trials, how to make it well ?
Know we the limit of the power He gives
To lesser Wills to will imperfectly ?
Is earth that limit ? Is the last link man,
Between the finite and the infinite ?
When that new star flared out in heaven, and died,
Who knows what Spirit, failing in his plan,
Dashed out his work in wrath, to try anew ?

O mother world ! we stammer at thy knee
Vainly our childish questions. 'T is enough
For such as we to know, that on His throne,
Nearer than we can think, and farther off
Than any mind can fathom, sits the One,
And sees to it — though pain and evil come,
And all may not be good — that all is well.

SEMELE

What were the garden-bowers of Thebes to
    me ?
What cared I for their dances and their feasts,
Whose heart awaited an immortal doom ?
The Greek youths mocked me, since I shunned in
    scorn
Them and their praises of my brows and hair.
The light girls pointed after me, who turned
Soul-sick from their unending fooleries.
Apollo's noon-glare wrathfully beat down
Upon the head that would not bend to him —
Him in his fuming anger ! — as the highest.
In every lily's cup a venomous thing
Crooked up its hairy limbs; or, if I bent
To pluck a blue-eyed blossom in the grass,
Some squatted horror leered with motionless eyes.

I think the very earth did hate my feet,
And put forth thistles to them, since I loathed
Her bare brown bosom; and the scowling pines
Menaced me with dark arms, and hissed their threats
Behind me, hurrying through their gloom, to watch
(Blurred in unsteady tears till all their beams
Dazzled, and shrank, and grew) that oval ring
Of shining points that rift the Milky Way,

Revealing, through their gap in the dusted fire,
The hollow awfulness of night beyond.

———————

There came a change : a glory fell to me.
No more 't was Semele, the lonely girl,
But Jupiter's Beloved, Semele.
With human arms the god came clasping me :
New life streamed from his presence ; and a voice
That scarce could curb itself to the smooth Greek
Now and anon swept forth in those deep nights,
Thrilling my flesh with awe ; mysterious words —
I knew not what ; hints of unearthly things
That I had felt on solemn summer noons,
When sleeping earth dreamed music, and the heart
Went crooning a low song it could not learn,
But wandered over it, as one who gropes
For a forgotten chord upon a lyre.

———————

Yea, Jupiter ! But why this mortal guise,
Wooing as if he were a milk-faced boy ?
Did I lack lovers ? Was my beauty dulled,
The golden hair turned dross, the lithe limbs shrunk,
The deathless longings tamed, that I should seethe
My soul in love like any shepherd girl ?
One night he sware to grant whate'er I asked ;
And straight I cried, " To know thee as thou art !
To hold thee on my heart as Juno does !

Come in thy thunder — kill me with one fierce
Divine embrace! Thine oath! — Now, Earth, at
    last!"

  The heavens shot one swift sheet of lurid flame:
The world crashed: from a body scathed and torn
The soul leapt through, and found his breast, and died.
  "Died?" — So the Theban maidens think, and
    laugh,
Saying, "She had her wish, that Semele!"
But sitting here upon Olympus' height
I look down, through that oval ring of stars,
And see the far-off Earth, a twinkling speck —
Dust-mote whirled up from the Sun's chariot-wheel —
And pity their small hearts that hold a man
As if he were a god; or know the god —
Or dare to know him — only as a man!
— O human love, art thou forever blind?

CLASS SONG

1864

As through the noon the reapers rest,
Till sinks the sun adown the west,
From morning toil an hour we come
To dream beneath the trees of home.

O gentle elms, within your shade
Ye keep the vows that we have made:
Your bending boughs, in tender tone,
Are whispering still of Sixty-One.

Like drowsy murmurs of the noon,
Our noisy futures melt in tune,
And all the past, like ocean shell,
Still echoing, sighs — farewell, farewell!

Pure as the evening's pearly star,
And sweet as songs that float afar,
Our olden love comes back to-night,
In music soft, and starry light.

O summer wind, on pinions strong,
Waft to the absent ones our song;
And tell them, wander as they will,
We love them still, — we love them still!

THE GAME OF LIFE

WE are living a game of chess, dear May —
For the prize of the *Better Life* we play.
The wonderful world is our chequered board,
And our hearts the box where the pieces are stored.
  The evil one has ever been
  Our foe, and uses our faults for men.
There's the Black King *Fear* and the Black Queen
     Pride
With her bishops *Envy* and *Spite* beside,
And his knights are *Malice* and *Deceit*,
His castles *Stubbornness* and *Hate*,
And for pawns each little idle sin,
That trusts to its smallness to creep, creeps in.

But on our side the white King, *Will*,
And the white Queen *Love*, march conquering still.
Her bishops are *Honor* and *Purity*,
Her knights are *Kindness* and *Charity*,
And for castles staunch and strong and fair,
Courage and *Constancy* are there,
And the little pawns to be given away
Are our little kindly acts each day.
Sometimes a wily foe is met
And the wavering will is sore beset ;

But we do not fight quite all alone —
There comes a quiet whispered tone,
An unseen touch that seems to fall
In answer to the faintest call,
And lifts our fingers tired and lame,
And points the move that wins the game.
In dazzling day or blinding night
God ne'er forgets us in the fight;
His glorious angels will abide
If we but clasp them at our side;
The hand that beckons them is Prayer,
And Faith the clasp that holds them there.

MAN, THE SPIRIT

A SMALL, swift planet, glimmering round a star, —
A molten drop with thinnest crusted shell
Of lime and flint, roofed-in with azure air, —
A winding stair of life, from Trilobite
And Saurian up to one who walks their king,
Drawing the lime and flint up through themselves
And kindling them to spirit, till on him,
Whose limbs are clay, there flames a lambent crown
Of fire from heaven, — these make our world.

         What then
Is this wild creature, wandering up and down,
Seeking a thousand things, but keeping still
A thought of God in his heart ? Why is he here,
Feet in the sod and thoughts among the stars,
Bewildered for some watchword or command,
As a battalion wavering on the field
Without a leader ?   In the march of worlds
Is Earth alone forgotten ?

        Who are we,
Clustered to-day with eyes and hands that clasp
As by some secret oath of brotherhood,
Out of the mass that jostles to and fro

Forever, without aim or hope ?   We are pledged
To UNDERSTAND, to live the truth we know,
And help men so to live and understand.
A handful 'gainst a host, we make our stand,
Nailing this thesis on the golden gate
Of the new Mammon-temples — that the souls —
The striving, praying, hoping, human souls —
Alone on earth are valuable — their end
To will God's will, because their will belongs
To him, the maker and the giver, so
Dilating to the broader destiny
Whose shadowy gateway opens from our world.

Out of the wrinkled bosom of the Old,
New England once was born ; a rock-hewn race,
Puritan pilgrims, splendidly pure and grim.
Flint-set against all sham, they rose to say
'T was sunrise and the ghosts must vanish now
Before the living Fact : that a king's crowned head
Was but a man's head, and it must come off
Like any beggar's, when it wrought a wrong.
They freed society, the individual man
We must emancipate ; they stripped all masks,
And knocked the fool's-caps off the venerable heads
Of church and state, and tore their pompous robes
To strings for children to fly kites with.

Here
Upon a coast whose calmer-blossoming surf
Beats not with such an iron clang as theirs,

We plant the Newer England; this our word,
That man is no mere spider-like machine
To spin out webs of railroads after him
In all earth's corners, nor a crafty brain
Made to knit cunning nets of politics
Or sharpen down to insignificance
On the grinding wheels of business, but a Soul,
That travelling higher worlds in upper light
Dips down through bodily contact into this;
As a hand trails over a boat's side through the
      waves,
And seems to the sea-creatures, eyed alone
For their own element, a thing of the sea.
Whether he wear the purple or the serge,
Whether he worship under frescoed pomp
Or bare-hewn rafters, it is still the man,
The individual spirit, something far
Beyond earth's chemistry, to whom all else
Are only foot-lights, scene, accessory,
Or nothing — or a farce, a mockery.

In this fair land, whose fields lie robed in bloom,
A living poem bound in blue and gold,
With azure flowers like little flecks of sky
Fallen, tangled in the dew-drops, to the grass,
And orange ones — as if the wealth below
Had blossomed up in beaten flakes of gold;
Where all the baser elements of earth,
Aspiring up through root, and stalk, and leaf,

Stand stretching delicate petal-wings toward heaven,
Poised on their slender feet for flying; here
Nature, like amorous Cleopatra, plots
To hold her Cæsar, brimming every sense
With perfume, song, and gorgeous coloring,
Throws softly wooing winds about his neck,
With sparkling air (as tho' not pearls alone,
But diamonds were dissolved in it), still fires
His brain to seek new dalliance, fresh delight,
Forgetful of his throne beyond the Sea.
Content with the golden Present, now, they say,
We must pore in the past no longer; our old books,
And antique, moss-grown system must give way
To the new patent methods for the mind;
New patent lives to lead, with no more dreams
And superstitions, only practical work.
A callow-winged philosophy breaks shell
And cackles prematurely loud that we
Are mummied, gone behind the times; no more
Dead languages, nor cloister-life — the lore
That will not take the harness for their use,
To weave, or grind, or burrow-out the mine,
Smells mouldy to their noses — Sophomores,
And *parvenus* of the intellectual world!
Who would brush down from heaven the olden
        stars,
To set new, self-adjusting spangles there,
Would mow the everlasting mountains off,
And build up straight, right-angled ones instead.

What is our training — what do colleges give
To men, which makes that feared and sneered-at
        thing,
A culture through the classics ?   Do we dare
Reveal the Eleusinian mysteries
Which leave such impress on these white boy-brows,
That the world, recognizing kingship, says,
" Here is a soul that knows itself, has touched
The centre, and radiates the broadening beams
Of influence straight to the point he means " ?
We cannot, if we would, tell all ; we hold
Some things there are that never can be told.

Articulate speech is but a coarse-woven sieve
That drops the fine gold through ; some subtile chords
Of swift and ravishing music lurk *between*
The written notes.   This only we can tell :
The boy, clear-eyed and beautiful-browed, is led
To a quiet spot arched over by great trees,
And this seal set upon him, — for four years
Sacred from all the tarnishing touch of men ;
Shut from the jangling of the brazen bells
That strike the hours of the Present noisily,
He is bid to listen — and along the years
Float up the echoes of the Past, the world's
Birth-songs and marching-music, requiems and prayers.
He learns the languages that we call " dead "
(The only living ones, whose fire still glows
Beneath the ash of every modern tongue),

The scrolls that men have dabbled with heart's blood,
Blotted with tears, are his, to learn that all
Is accident and flying form except the soul.
The outer husk, the crown, the robes, or rags
Signify nothing; Roman, Greek, and Goth,
Ate, slept, and dreamed, and died, like modern men.
The audible word is nothing — if the lips
Prayed Zeus or Allah, Elohim or Lord,
The heart said still the same.   He learns to choose
The changeless from the changing, as sole good.
Only the trivial chaff is fanned away,
As Time's broad wings go sweeping over earth.
The futile acquisitions of to-day
Tempt him but little, so the heart grow full
With inner force and outward-burning fire.
No surface buckling-on of glittering facts
His mind would have, but weapons that can make
The sinewy arm to wield them; for the sword
And shield will moulder, but the sinewy arm
Has many a field to fight beyond this earth.

Stretched under some cathedral-roof of elm,
Frescoed in flickering sunlights, with far eyes
That watch and do not see the summer sky —
A cloudy opal, veined as when a wave
Leaps up, and breaks, and leaves the milk-white
            foam
Streaking its meshes over the blue sea —
Flat to the ground, where he can seem to feel

The great earth heave beneath him like a ship
Plunging its course along the tideless space,
He whispers with his heart in thoughts like these:

THE FUTURE

What may we take into the vast Forever?
      That marble door
Admits no fruit of all our long endeavor,
        No fame-wreathed crown we wore,
        No garnered lore.

What can we bear beyond the unknown portal?
      No gold, no gains
Of all our toiling, in the life immortal
        No hoarded wealth remains,
        Nor gilds, nor stains.

Naked from out that far abyss behind us
      We entered here:
No word came with our coming to remind us
        What wondrous world was near,
        No hope, no fear.

Into the silent, starless Night before us,
      Naked we glide:
No hand has mapped the constellations o'er us,
        No comrade at our side,
        No chart, no guide.

Yet fearless toward that midnight, black and hollow,
      Our footsteps fare:
The beckoning of a father's hand we follow,
      His love alone is there,
      No curse, no care.

    And so we learn our world, finding how time
Is an illusion — the perspective all
But a mere trick of shadow, which can make
That misty peak seem far beyond the hill
In the foreground — touch it, and you see
'T is all one whole: The Greek stands at our side,
Toga and sandals shielding the same flesh
That coat and shoes do now, the same hot brain
Throbbing beneath the helmet as the hat.
As one who hums a tune about his work,
And hears a friend's voice from another room
Strike in an alto, so we hear afar
The sound of voices all along the past
Chording with ours. 'T was only yesterday
That Plato stood and talked with Socrates;
'T was last night Paul was here, and on the desk
He left his letters, which the air has turned
From parchment into paper for our use.
In the next room they wait; 't is but a step
Over the threshold to them there, yet since
The shadow of the tree of life lies dark
Across the doorway, like a faltering child

We dread the passage through the cold dark hall,
To where the Father calls, and they have gone.

What is the visible, tangible world all worth,
Except for symbols, somewhat coarse and large,
Like the raised letters for the blind to feel?
The shadowy domes serenely lifted up,
The soundless depths that deepen down in thought,
Make one small world draw dwindling to a point.
The little earth! Think, that the same bright sun,
Which rises there from the familiar hill
And laughs its level joy straight to our eyes,
Is wrapping half the globe in morning light,
Kindling dew-diamonds on the tropic palm,
Tipping the white gull's wing o'er Northern seas
And striking frozen fire from the iceberg's towers
At either pole.

                    The brisk and dapper minds
Are doubtless those which have had the practical
And not the philosophic training, yet
When the world wants a great man for great deeds,
Who ever took the modern-fashioned one,
Who had learned the useful only and eschewed
Dead languages or dreaming in the woods?
The great man ever has sought the sacred fire
From olden books, or from the older stars
In solitudes, away from the bustling streets
And babbling men.

> Ah, who can speak of great
Nor think of him who was our greatest one ?
Let us wait here, and lay a wreath of song
Upon our grave.

THE DEAD PRESIDENT

Were there no crowns on earth,
No evergreen to weave a hero's wreath,
That he must pass beyond the gates of death,
Our hero, our slain hero, to be crowned ?
Could there on our unworthy earth be found
  Naught to befit his worth ?

The noblest soul of all !
When was there ever, since our Washington,
A man so pure, so wise, so patient — one
Who walked with this high goal alone in sight,
To speak, to do, to sanction only Right,
  Though very heaven should fall !

Ah, not for him we weep ;
What honor more could be in store for him ?
Who would have had him linger in our dim
And troublesome world, when his great work was done ?
Who would not leave that worn and weary one
  Gladly to go to sleep ?

For us the stroke was just ;
We were not worthy of that patient heart ;

We might have helped him more, not stood apart,
And coldly criticised his works and ways —
Too late now, all too late — our little praise
　　Sounds hollow o'er his dust.

　　Be merciful, O our God !
Forgive the meanness of our human hearts,
That never, till a noble soul departs,
See half the worth, or hear the angel's wings
Till they go rustling heavenward as he springs
　　Up from the mounded sod.

　　Yet what a deathless crown
Of Northern pine and Southern orange-flower,
For victory, and the land's new bridal hour,
Would we have wreathed for that beloved brow !
Sadly upon his sleeping forehead now
　　We lay our cypress down.

　　O martyred one, farewell !
Thou hast not left thy people quite alone,
Out of thy beautiful life there comes a tone
Of power, of love, of trust, a prophecy,
Whose fair fulfillment all the earth shall be,
　　And all the Future tell.

————

　　Earth's greatest ones ever have gone so far
Out on life's borderland, that they have caught
The sound of an infinite ocean, far away,

Rounding our island-world. But now appear
These new philosophers, practical, well-informed,
Assuring us there is no ocean-sound —
'T is but the roaring in our feverish ears.
They carry the glimmering lantern of conceit
Swinging along their path, and see no Night,
No fathomless, sombre glory of the dark,
But their own shadows, that seem giant forms,
Stalking across the fields and fences — they
That are stumbling pygmies!

                        They will show you God
And all his universe in a nutshell : see!
Pinched in our little theory like a vice,
We cleave the nut with a keen hypothesis,
Whisk off the top — there 't is convenient
For logical handling. " Cannot see ? " Oh, then
You have spoiled your eyes with gazing at the sun.
Hard, angular, and dry, they pish and pooh
At all ideas they cannot measure off
And pack into their iron-bound, narrow brain.
They 'll not admit the existence of a truth
Which cannot be expressed in x and y,
And solved by their quadratics. Well, they serve
To show a new phenomenon in the world :
That a mind, if taken in time, can be transformed
To a machine of clockwork, cogs and wheels
Wound up with useful facts, and set away
On a shelf to go its narrow round of thought

And tell us when 't is noon or supper time,
If we get careless through abstraction. So
All men, even these, have uses. Some to go
Whirling around the circumference
Spinning out sparks into the darkling space,
While some sit staidly at the safe, slow hub
And swear there are no radii and no rim,
No winged steeds far at the chariot's pole,
No Power that rides, triumphant, terrible.
What has this new, pert century done for man,
That it affords to sneer at all before,
Because it rides its aimless jaunts by steam
And blabs its trivial talk by telegraph?
What of it? Are not babes born naked now,
As ever, and go naked from the world?
If I am the ape's cousin, what to me
Are steam and harnessed lightning, art and law?
If the night comes on so soon, what matters it
If the short day be foul or fair — if Fate
Rain thunderbolts or roses on our heads?
Yea, even 't were some satisfaction then
To stand and take the thunderbolts, and think
We are large enough at least to serve as marks
For gods to hurl at.

              If there is no key,
Why puzzle longer with the scribbled scroll
We blur our eyes on? But, O merciful God,
If our souls are immortal, O forgive

That we still creep on dusty hands and knees,
Face downward to the ground, when we might
      walk
Erect, and face the heavens, and see thy stars!

We gaze from our separate windows on the Night
And find our own small faces imaged there
In the glass, nor ever see the shadowy plain
Stretching out through the dimness, on and on.

Splendid beginners, still we toil and fill
The vestibule of our lives with useless plans,
With noise of hammer, scaffolding and dust
And rubbish, building some imagined fane
To worship in through years that never come.
For life is like the legendary bird
The Christ-child's hands were moulding out of
      clay:
While we are shaping it with eager care,
We look up startled, for the bird has flown!

Ah, if the mind could sometimes be content
To cease from its male madness, its desire
To radiate outward, and in passive rest
Receive from Nature's ever-waiting arms
Energy, fire, and life! We blind ourselves
With briny sweat-drops, even more than tears.
Ever with burning haste we scorch our souls,
And set their compass-needles whirring round

So they can never keenly point to the pole.
There's such a clash and jar kept up within,
Hissing of nerve-steam, iron purposes
Clanging on one another, who can hear
The sweet, sweet silver voices from afar?
Ah, let a man but listen! Have we not
Two ears for silence, one small mouth for noise?
Listen until we catch the key, and know
Our note, and then chime in — not rave and run,
And shout our frantic orders, just as though
We were the leader of the orchestra,
Not little separate voices; could we wait,
Each in his corner, conning quietly
His part, the chords would be the sweeter for it.

A PARADOX

Haste, haste, O laggard — leave thy drowsy dreams!
Cram all thy brain with knowledge; clutch and
        cram!
The earth is wide, the universe is vast:
Thou hast infinity to learn. Oh, haste!

Haste not, haste not, my soul! "Infinity"?
Thou hast eternity to learn it in.
Thy boundless lesson through the endless years
Hath boundless leisure. Run not like a slave —
Sit like a king, and see the ranks of worlds
Wheel in their cycles onward to thy feet.

HOME

I know a spot beneath three ancient trees,
    A solitude of green and grassy shade,
Where the tall roses, naked to the knees,
    In that deep shadow wade,
Whose rippled coolness drips from bough to bough,
And bathes the world's vexation from my brow.

The gnarléd limbs spring upward airy-free,
    And from their perfect arch they scarcely swerve,
Like spouted fountains from a dark, green sea
    So beautiful they curve, —
Motionless fountains, slumbering in mid-air,
With spray of shadows falling everywhere.

Here the Sun comes not like the king of day,
    To rule his own, but hesitant, afraid,
Forbears his sceptre's golden length to lay
    Across the inviolate shade,
And wraps the broad space like a darkened tent,
With many a quivering shaft of splendor rent.

Seclusion, as an island still and lone,
    Round which the ocean-world may ebb and flow,
Unheeded, following fruitlessly the moon,
    And where the soul may go
Naked of all its vanities and cares,
To meet the bounteous grace that Nature bares.

Here stretched at morn I watch the sunrise ray
　　That sweeps across the earth like minstrel's hand,
Waking from all the birds a song of day,
　　Caught up from land to land,
And earth is beautiful and hearts are brave,
Ere busy Life has waked to claim her slave.

Each day a pure and velvet-petal'd flower,
　　Blooms fresh at dawn, with trembling light be-
　　　　dewn,
But dull and tarnished at the mid-day hour —
　　The noisy, trampling noon,
Its beauty soiled with handling. Ever choose
The virgin morning for the soul to use.

The wind comes hushing, hushing through the trees
　　Like surf that breaks on an invisible beach
And sends a spray of whispers down the breeze,
　　Whispers that seem to reach
From some far inner land where spirits dwell,
And hint the secret which they may not tell.

No garrulous company is here, but books —
　　Earth's best men taken at their best — books
　　　　used,
With dark-edged paths, and penciled margin-strokes,
　　Where friends have paused and mused,
And here and there beneath the noticed lines,
Faint zigzag marks like little trailing vines.

Here what to me are all the childish cares
    That make a Bedlam of the busy world?
Each hour that flies some quiet message bears
    Beneath its moments furled,
Like a white dove, that, under her soft wings,
Kind thoughts from far-off home and kindred brings.

  So let us live, not pent in noisy towns,
But in calm places, watching all things fair —
The months following in waves across the fields,
Each stranding there new flowery pearls and shells;
The flocks of shadows nestled 'neath the trees;
The laughing brooks, like mischievous children still
Tangling the silver thread of the motherly moon.
So shall Earth be no more a theatre,
In which a tragic comedy is played —
A horrible farce with too real murder in it —
But a fair field where till the break of day
Man wrestles with the Angel of his fate
For an immortal blessing.
               If we knew,
O Father, if we knew we die not, but
Live on, we should live worthier of thy love:
So help thy little ones to know and live:
That as a shadow which goes reaching forth
Longer and longer as the sun goes down,
The soul may stretch forth toward the great Unseen,
Until the sacred, solemn starlight comes
Gathering our individual shadows in its own.

THE CHOICE

ONLY so much of power each day —
So much nerve-force brought in play;
If it goes for politics or trade,
Ends gained or money made,
You have it not for the soul and God —
The choice is yours, to soar or plod.
So much water in the rill:
It may go to turn the miller's wheel,
    Or sink in the desert, or flow on free
To brighten its banks in meadows green,
Till broadening out, fair fields between,
    It streams to the moon-enchanted sea.
Only so little power each day:
Week by week days slide away;
    Ere the life goes, what shall it be —
A trade — a game — a mockery,
Or the gate of a rich Eternity?

WISDOM AND FAME

A WILDERNESS, made awful with the night —
Great glimmering trunks whose tops were hid in
      gloom,
Vast columns in the blackness broken off,
Between whose ghostly forms, slow-wandering,
A company of lost men sought a path.
    Some groped among the dead leaves and fallen
        boughs
For footprints; but the rattle of the leaves
And crook of stems seemed serpents coiled to strike
    Some took the momentary sparks that rode
Upon their straining eyeballs, for far lights,
And followed them.
            Some stood apart, in vain
Searching, with horror-widened eyes, for stars.
    So, stumbling on, they circled round and round
Through the same mazes.
             Then they singled one
To climb a pinnacled height, and see from thence
The landmarks, and to shout from thence their course.
With aching sinews, bleeding feet, bruised hands,
He gained the height; but when they cried to him
They got but maudlin answers, — he had found,
Slaking hot thirst, a fruit that maddened him.

Another, and another still they sent;
But every one that climbed found the ill fruit
And maddened, and gave back but wild replies:
And still in darkness they go wandering, lost.

SERENITY

BROOK,
Be still, — be still!
Midnight's arch is broken
In thy ceaseless ripples.
Dark and cold below them
Runs the troubled water, —
Only on its bosom,
Shimmering and trembling,
Doth the glinted star-shine
    Sparkle and cease.

Life,
Be still, — be still!
Boundless truth is shattered
On thy hurrying current.
Rest, with face uplifted,
Calm, serenely quiet;
Drink the deathless beauty —
Thrills of love and wonder
Sinking, shining, star-like;
Till the mirrored heaven
Hollow down within thee
Holy deeps unfathomed,
Where far thoughts go floating,
And low voices wander
    Whispering peace.

THE HERMITAGE, AND OTHER POEMS

THE HERMITAGE

CALIFORNIA, BAY OF SAN FRANCISCO, 1866

I

A LIFE, — a common, cleanly, quiet life,
Full of good citizenship and repute,
New, but with promise of prosperity, —
A well-bred, fair, young-gentlemanly life, —
What business had a girl to bring her eyes,
And her blonde hair, and her clear, ringing voice,
And break up life, as a bell breaks a dream?
Had Love Christ's wrath, and did this life sell doves
In the world's temple, that Love scourged it forth
Beyond the gates? Within, the worshipers, —
Without, the waste, and the hill-country, where
The life, with smarting shoulders and stung heart,
Unknowing that the hand which scourged could
        heal,
Drave forth, blind, cursing, in despair to die,
Or work its own salvation out in fear.

Copyright, 1904, by the Detroit Photographic Co.

SAN FRANCISCO BAY, CALIFORNIA

Old World — old, foolish, wicked World — fare-
    well!
Since the Time-angel left my soul with thee,
Thou hast been a hard stepmother unto me.
Now I at last rebel
Against thy stony eyes and cruel hands.
I will go seek in far-off lands
Some quiet corner, where my years shall be
Still as the shadow of a brooding bird
That stirs but with her heart-beats. Far, unheard
May wrangle on the noisy human host,
While I will face my Life, that silent ghost,
And force it speak what it would have with me.

   Not of the fair young Earth,
The snow-crowned, sunny-belted globe;
Not of its skies, nor Twilight's purple robe,
Nor pearly dawn; not of the flowers' birth,
And Autumn's forest-funerals; not of storms,
And quiet seas, and clouds' incessant forms;
Not of the sanctuary of the night,
With its solemnities, nor any sight
And pleasant sound of all the friendly day:
But I am tired of what we call our lives;
Tired of the endless humming in the hives, —
Sick of the bitter honey that we eat,
And sick of cursing all the shallow cheat.

   Let me arise, and away
To the land that guards the dying day,

Whose burning tear, the evening-star,
Drops silently to the wave afar;
The land where summers never cease
Their sunny psalm of light and peace.
Whose moonlight, poured for years untold,
Has drifted down in dust of gold;
Whose morning splendors, fallen in showers,
Leave ceaseless sunrise in the flowers.

There I will choose some eyrie in the hills,
Where I may build, like a lonely bird,
And catch the whispered music heard
Out of the noise of human ills.

So, I am here at last;
A purer world, whose feet the old, salt Past
Washes against, and leaves it fresh and free
As a new island risen from the sea.

Three dreamy weeks we lay on Ocean's breast,
Rocked asleep, by gentle winds caressed,
Or crooned with wild wave-lullabies to rest.
A memory of foam and glassy spray;
Wave chasing wave, like young sea-beasts at play;
Stretches of misty silver 'neath the moon,
And night-airs murmuring many a quiet tune.
Three long, delicious weeks' monotony
Of sky, and stars, and sea,

Broken midway by one day's tropic scene
Of giant plants, tangles of luminous green,
With fiery flowers and purple fruits between.

    I have found a spot for my hermitage, —
No dank and sunless cave, —
I come not for a dungeon, nor a cage, —
Not to be Nature's slave,
But, as a weary child,
Unto the mother's faithful arms I flee,
And seek the sunniest footstool at her knee,
Where I may sit beneath caresses mild,
And hear the sweet old songs that she will sing to me.

    'T is a grassy mountain-nook,
In a gorge, whose foaming brook
Tumbles through from the heights above,
Merrily leaping to the light
From the pine-wood's haunted gloom, —
As a romping child,
Affrighted, from a sombre room
Leaps to the sunshine, laughing with delight:
Be this my home, by man's tread undefiled.
Here sounds no voice but of the mourning dove,
Nor harsher footsteps on the sands appear
Than the sharp, slender hoof-marks of the deer,
Or where the quail has left a zigzag row
Of lightly printed stars her track to show.

Above me frowns a front of rocky wall,
Deep cloven into ruined pillars tall
And sculptures strange; bald to its dizzy edge,
Save where, in some deep crevice of a ledge
Buttressed by its black shadow hung below,
A solitary pine has cleft the rock, —
Straight as an arrow, feathered to the tip,
As if a shaft from the moon-huntress' bow
Had struck and grazed the cliff's defiant lip,
And stood, still stiffly quivering with the shock.

Beyond the gorge a slope runs half-way up,
With hollow curve as for a giant's cup,
Brimming with blue pine-shadows: then in air
The gray rock rises bare,
Its front deep-fluted by the sculptor-storms
In moulded columns, rounded forms,
As if great organ-pipes were chiseled there,
Whose anthems are the torrent's roar below,
And chanting winds that through the pine-tops go.
Here bursts of requiem music sink and rise,
When the full moonlight, slowly streaming, lies
Like panes of gold on some cathedral pave,
While floating mists their silver incense wave,
And from on high, through fleecy window-bars,
Gaze down the saintly faces of the stars.

Against the huge trunk of a storm-snapped tree,
(Whose hollow, ready-hewn by long decay,

Above, a chimney, lined with slate and clay,
Below, a broad-arched fireplace makes for me,)
I 've built of saplings and long limbs a hut.
The roof with lacing boughs is tightly shut,
Thatched with thick-spreading palms of pine,
And tangled over by a wandering vine,
Uprooted from the woods close by,
Whose clasping tendrils climb and twine,
Waving their little hands on high,
As if they loved to deck this nest of mine.
Within, by smooth white stones from the brook's beach
My rooms are separated, each from each.
On yonder island-rock my table 's spread,
Brook-ringed, that no stray, fasting ant may come
To make himself with my wild fare at home.

Here will I live, and here my life shall be
Serene, still, rooted steadfastly,
Yet pointing skyward, and its motions keep
A rhythmic balance, as that cedar tall,
Whose straight shaft rises from the chasm there,
Through the blue, hollow air,
And, measuring the dizzy deep,
Leans its long shadow on the rock's gray wall.

———

Through the sharp gap of the gorge below,
From my mountains' feet the gaze may go
Over a stretch of fields, broad-sunned,
Then glance beyond,

Across the beautiful bay,
To that dim ridge, a score of miles away,
Lifting its clear-cut outline high,
Azure with distance on the azure sky,
Whose flocks of white clouds brooding on its crests
Have winged from ocean to their piny nests.
Beyond the bright blue water's further rim,
Where waves seem ripples on its far-off brim,
The rich young city lies,
Diminished to an ant-hill's size.
I trace its steep streets, ribbing all the hill
Like narrow bands of steel,
Binding the city on the shifting sand :
Thick-pressed between them stand
Broad piles of buildings, pricked through here and
     there
By a sharp steeple ; and above, the air
Murky with smoke and dust, that seem to show
The bright sky saddened by the sin below.

   The voice of my wild brook is marvelous ;
Leaning above it from a jutting rock
To watch the image of my face, that forms
And breaks, and forms again (as the image of God
Is broken and re-gathered in a soul),
I listen to the chords that sink and swell
From many a little fall and babbling run.
That hollow gurgle is the deepest bass ;

Over the pebbles gush contralto tones,
While shriller trebles tinkle merrily,
Running, like some enchanted-fingered flute,
Endless chromatics.
            Now it is the hum
And roar of distant streets; the rush of winds
Through far-off forests: now the noise of rain
Drumming the roof; the hiss of ocean-foam:
Now the swift ripple of piano-keys
In mad mazurkas, danced by laughing girls.

So, night and day, the hurrying brook goes on;
Sometimes in noisy glee, sometimes far down,
Silent along the bottom of the gorge,
Like a deep passion hidden in the soul,
That chafes in secret hunger for its sea: .
Yet not so still but that heaven finds its course;
And not so hid but that the yearning night
Broods over it, and feeds it with her stars.

———

When earth has Eden spots like this for man,
Why will he drag his life where lashing storms
Whip him indoors, the petulant weather's slave?
There he is but a helpless, naked snail,
Except he wear his house close at his back.
Here the wide air builds him his palace walls, —
Some little corner of it roofed, for sleep;
Or he can lie all night, bare to the sky,

And feel updrawn against the breast of heaven,
Letting his thoughts stretch out among the stars,
As the antennæ of an insect grope
Blindly for food, or as the ivy's shoots
Clamber from cope and tower to find the light,
And drink the electric pulses of the sun.

As from that sun we draw the coarser fire
That swells the veins, and builds the brain and
     bone,
So from each star a finer influence streams,
Kindling within the mortal chrysalis
The first faint thrills of its new life to come.

Here is no niggard gap of sky above,
With murk and mist below, but all sides clear, —
Not an inch bated from the full-swung dome;
Each constellation to the horizon's rim
Keen-glittering, as if one only need
Walk to the edge there, spread his wings, and float,
The dark earth spurned behind, into the blue.

———————

I love thee, thou brown, homely, dear old Earth!
Those fairer planets whither fate may lead,
Whatever marvel be their bulk or speed,
Ringed with what splendor, belted round with fire,
In glory of perpetual moons arrayed,
Can ne'er give back the glow and fresh desire
Of youth in that old home where man had birth,

Whose paths he trod through wholesome light and
    shade.
Out of their silver radiance to thy dim
And clouded orb his eye will turn,
As an old man looks back to where he played
About his father's hearth, and finds for him
No splendor like the fires which there did burn.

See: I am come to live alone with thee.
Thou hast had many a one, grown old and worn,
Come to thee weary and forlorn,
Bent with the weight of human vanity.
But I come with my life almost untried,
In thy perpetual presence to abide.
Teach me thy wisdom; let me learn the flowers,
And know the rocks and trees,
And touch the springs of all thy hidden powers.
Let the still gloom of thy rock-fastnesses
Fall deep upon my spirit, till the voice
Of brooks become familiar, and my heart rejoice
With joy of birds and winds; and all the hours,
Unmaddened by the babble of vain men,
Bring thy most inner converse to my ken.
So shall it be, that, when I stand
On that next planet's ruddy-shimmering strand,
I shall not seem a pert and forward child
Seeking to dabble in abstruser lore
With alphabet unlearned, who in disgrace
Returns, upon his primer yet to pore —

But those examiners, all wise and mild,
Shall gently lead me to my place,
As one that faithfully did trace
These simpler earthly records o'er and o'er.

———

Beckoned at sunrise by the surf's white hand,
I have strayed down to sit upon the beach,
And hear the oratorio of the Sea.
On this steep, crumbling bank, where the high
    tides
Have crunched the earth away, a crooked oak —
A hunch-backed dwarf, whose limbs, cramped down
    by gales,
Have twisted stiffening back upon themselves —
Spreads me a little arbor from the sun.

On the brown, shining beach, all ripple-carved,
Gleams now and then a pool; so smooth and
    clear,
That, though I cannot see the plover there
Pacing its farther edge (so much he looks
The color of the sand), yet I can trace
His image hanging in the glassy brine —
Slim legs and rapier-beak — like silver-plate
With such a pictured bird clean-etched upon it.

Beyond, long curves of little shallow waves
Creep, tremulous with ripples, to the shore,

GLEAMS NOW AND THEN A POOL SO SMOOTH AND CLEAR

Till the whole bay seems slowly sliding in,
With edge of snow that melts against the sand.

Above its twinkling blue, where ceaselessly
The white curve of a slender arm of foam
Is reached along the water, and withdrawn,
A flock of sea-birds darken into specks;
Then whiten, as they wheel with sunlit wings,
Winking and wavering against the sky.

The earth for form, the sea for coloring,
And overhead, fair daughters of the two,
The clouds, whose curves were moulded on the hills,
Whose tints of pearl and foam the ocean gave.

O Sea, thou art all-beautiful, but dumb!
Thou hast no utterance articulate
For human ears; only a restless moan
Of barren tides, that loathe the living earth
As alien, striving towards the barren moon.
Thou art no longer infinite to man:
Has he not touched thy boundary-shores, and now
Laid his electric fetters round thy feet?
Thy dumb moan saddens me; let me go back
And listen to the silence of the hills.

At last I live alone:
No human judgment-seats are here

Thrust in between man and his Maker's throne,
With praise to covet, or with frown to fear :
No small, distorted judgments bless, or blame ;
Only to Him I own
The inward sense of worth, or flush of shame.

God made the man alone ;
And all that first grand morning walked he so.
Then was he strong and wise, till at the noon,
When tired with joyous wonder he lay prone
For rest and sleep, God let him know
The subtile sweetness that is bound in Two.

Man rises best alone :
Upward his thoughts stream, like the leaping flame,
Whose base is tempest-blown ;
Upward and skyward, since from thence they came,
And thither they must flow.
But when in twos we go,
The lightnings of the brain weave to and fro,
Level across the abyss that parts us all ;
If upward, only slantwise, as we scale
Slowly together that night-shrouded wall
Which bounds our reason, lest our reason fail.
If linked in threes, and fives,
However heavenward the spirit strives,
The lowest stature draws the highest down, —
The king must keep the level of the clown.
The grosser matter has the greater power

In all attraction; every hour
We slide and slip to lower scales,
Till weary aspiration fails,
And that keen fire which might have pierced the
         skies
Is quenched and killed in one another's eyes.

A child had blown a bubble fair
That floated in the sunny air:
A hundred rainbows danced and swung
Upon its surface, as it hung
In films of changing color rolled,
Crimson, and amethyst, and gold,
With faintest streaks of azure sheen,
And curdling rivulets of green.
"If so the surface shines," cried he,
"What marvel must the centre be!"
He caught it — on his empty hands
A drop of turbid water stands!

With men, to help the moments fly,
I tossed the ball of talk on high,
With glancing jest, and random stings,
Grazing the crests of thoughts and things,
In many a shifting ray of speech
That shot swift sparkles, each to each.
I thought, "Ah, could we pierce below
To inner soul, what depths would show!"

In friendships many, loves a few,
I pierced the inner depths, and knew
'T was but the shell that splendor caught:
Within, one sour and selfish thought.

    I found a grotto, hidden in the gorge,
Paved by the brook in rare mosaic work
Of sand, and lucent depths, and shadow-streaks
Veining the amber of the sun-dyed wave.
Between two mossy masses of gray rock
Lay a clear basin, which, with sun and shade
Bewitched, a great transparent opal made,
Over whose broken rims the water ran.
Above each rocky side leaned waving trees
Whose lace of branches wove a restless roof,
Trailed over by green vines that sifted down
A dust of sunshine through the chilly shade.

    Leaning against a trunk of oak, rock-wedged,
Whose writhen roots were clenched upon the stones,
I was a Greek, and caught the sudden flash
Of a scared Dryad's vanishing robe, and heard
The laughter, half-suppressed, of hiding Fauns.
Up the dark stairway of the tumbling stream
The sun shot through, and struck each foamy fall
Into a silvery veil of dazzling fire.
Along its shady course, the tossing drops
By some swift sunbeam ever caught, were lit
To sparkling stars, that fell, and flashed, and fell,

Incessantly rekindled. Bubble-troops
Came dancing by, to break just at my feet ;
Lo ! every bubble mirrored the whole scene —
The streak of blue between the roofing-boughs,
And on it my own face in miniature
Quaintly distorted, as if some small elf
Peered up at me beneath his glassy dome.

If men but knew the mazes of the brain
And all its crowded pictures, they would need
No Louvre or Vatican : behind our brows
Intricate galleries are built, whose walls
Are rich with all the splendors of a life.
Each crimson leaf of every autumn walk,
Dewdrops of childhood's mornings, every scene
From any window where we 've chanced to stand,
Forgotten sunsets, summer afternoons,
Hang fresh in those immortal galleries.
Few ever can unlock them, till great Death
Unrolls our lifelong memory as a scroll.
One key is solitude, and silence one,
And one a quiet mind, content to rest
In God's sufficiency, and take His world,
Not dabbling all the Master's work to death
With our small interference. God is God.

Yet we must give the children leave to use
Our garden-tools, though they spoil tool and plant

In learning. So the Master may not scorn
Our awkwardness, as with these bungling hands
We try to uproot the ill, and plant with good
Life's barren soil: the child is learning use.
Perhaps the angels even are forbid
To laugh at us, or may not care to laugh,
With kind eyes pitying our little hurts.

'T is ludicrous that man should think he roams
Freely at will a world planned for his use.
Lo, what a mite he is! Snatched hither and yon,
Tossed round the sun, and in its orbit flashed
Round other centres, orbits without end;
His bit of brain too small to even feel
The spinning of the little hailstone, Earth.
So his creeds glibly prate of choice and will,
When his whole fate is an invisible speck
Whirled through the orbits of Eternity.

We think that we believe
That human souls shall live, and live,
When trees have rotted into mould,
And all the rocks which these long hills enfold
Have crumbled, and beneath new oceans lie.
But why — ah, why —
If puny man is not indeed to die,
Watch I with such disdain
That human speck creeping along the plain,

And turn with such a careless scorn of men
Back to the mountain's brow again,
And feel more pleased that some small, fluttering
    thing
Trusts me and hovers near on fearless wing,
Than if the proudest man in all the land
Had offered me in friendliness his hand?

   However small the present creature man, —
Ridiculous imitation of the gods,
Weak plagiarism on some completer world, —
Yet we can boast of that strong race to be.
The savage broke the attraction which binds fast
The fibres of the oak, and we to-day
By cunning chemistry can force apart
The elements of the air. That coming race
Shall loose the bands by which the earth attracts;
A drop of occult tincture, a spring touched
Shall outwit gravitation; men shall float,
Or lift the hills and set them where they will.
The savage crossed the lake, and we the sea.
That coming race shall have no bounds or bars,
But, like the fledgeling eaglet, leave the nest, —
Our earthly eyrie up among the stars, —
And freely soar, to tread the desolate moon,
Or mingle with the neighbor folk of Mars.
Yea, if the savage learned by sign and sound
To bridge the chasm to his fellow's brain,

Till now we flash our whispers round the globe,
That race shall signal over the abyss
To those bright souls who throng the outer courts
Of life, impatient who shall greet men first
And solve the riddles that we die to know.

———

'T is night : I sit alone among the hills.
There is no sound, except the sleepless brook,
Whose voice comes faintly from the depths below
Through the thick darkness, or the sombre pines
That slumber, murmuring sometimes in their dreams.
Hark! on a fitful gust there came the sound
Of the tide rising yonder on the bay.
It dies again : 't was like the rustling noise
Of a great army mustering secretly.
There rose an owl's cry, from the woods below,
Like a lost spirit's. — Now all 's still again. —
'T is almost fearful to sit here alone
And feel the deathly silence and the dark.
I will arise and shout, and hear at least
My own voice answer. — Not an echo even!
I wish I had not uttered that wild cry ;
It broke with such a shock upon the air,
Whose leaden silence closed up after it,
And seemed to clap together at my ears.
The black depths of these muffled woods are thronged
With shapes that wait some signal to swoop out,
And swirl around and madden me with fear.

I will go climb that bare and rocky height
Into the clearer air.

          So, here I breathe;
That silent darkness smothered me.
                      Away
Across the bay, the city with its lights
Twinkling against the horizon's dusky line,
Looks a sea-dragon, crawled up on the shore,
With rings of fire across his rounded back,
And luminous claws spread out among the hills.
Above, the glittering heavens. — Magnificent!
Oh, if a man could be but as a star,
Having his place appointed, here to rise,
And there to set, unchanged by earthly change,
Content if it can guide some wandering bark,
Or be a beacon to some homesick soul! ·

   Those city-lights again : they draw my gaze
As if some secret human sympathy
Still held my heart down from the lonely heaven.
A new-born constellation, settling there
Below the Sickle's ruby-hilted curve,
They gleam —— Not so! No constellation they;
I mock the sad, strong stars that never fail
In their eternal patience; from below
Comes that pale glare, like the faint, sulphurous flame
Which plays above the ashes of a fire :
So trembles the dull flicker of those lamps
Over the burnt-out energies of man.

II

A month since I last laid my pencil down, —
An April, fairer than the Atlantic June,
Whose calendar of perfect days was kept
By daily blossoming of some new flower.
The fields, whose carpets now were silken white,
Next week were orange-velvet, next, sea-blue.
It was as if some central fire of bloom,
From which in other climes a random root
Is now and then shot up, here had burst forth
And overflowed the fields, and set the land
Aflame with flowers.   I watched them day by day,
How at the dawn they wake, and open wide
Their little petal-windows, how they turn
Their slender necks to follow round the sun,
And how the passion they express all day
In burning color, steals forth with the dew
All night in odor.

                I have wandered much
These weeks, but everywhere a restless mind
Has dogged me like the shadow at my heels.
Sometimes I watched the morning mist arise,
Like an imprisoned Genie from the stream,
And wished that death would come on me like dawn,
Drawing the spirit, that white, vaporous mist,
Up from this noisy, fretted stream of life,
To fall where God will, in his bounteous showers.

Sometimes I walked at sunset on the edge
Of the steep gorge, and saw my shadow pace
Along a shadow-wall across the abyss,
And felt that we, with all our phantom deeds,
Are but far-slanted shadows of some life
That walks between our planet and its God.
All the long nights — those memory-haunted nights,
When sleepless conscience would not let me sleep,
But stung, and stung, and pointed to the world
Which like a coward I had left behind,
I watched the heavens, where week by week the moon
Slow swelled its silver bud, blossomed full gold,
And slowly faded.

        Laid the pencil down —
Why not? Are there not books enough? Is man
A sick child that must be amused by songs,
Or be made sicker with their foolish noise?

  Then illness came: I should have argued, once,
That the ill body gave me those ill thoughts;
But I have learned that spirit, though it be
Subtile, and hard to trace, is mightier
Than matter, and I know the poisoned mind
Poisoned its shell. Three days of fever-fire
Burned out my strength, leaving me scarcely power
To reach the brook's side and my scanty food.
What would I not have given to hear the voice
Of some one who would raise my throbbing head

And shade the fevering sun, and cool my hand
In her moist palms! But I lay there, alone.
Blessed be sickness, which cuts down our pride
And bares our helplessness. I have had new thoughts.
I think the fever burned away some lies
Which clogged the truthful currents of the brain.
Am I quite happy here? Have I the right,
As wholly independent, to scorn men?
What do I owe them — self? Should I be I,
Born in these hills? A savage rather! Food,
The sailor-bread? Yes, that took mill and men:
Yet flesh and fowl are free; but powder and gun —
What human lives went to the making of them?
I am dependent as the villager
Who lives by the white wagon's daily round.
Yea, better feed upon the ox, to which
The knife is mercy after slavery,
Than kill the innocent birds, and trustful deer
Whose big blue eyes have almost human pain;
That's murder!
　　　　　　　　I scorned books: to those same books
I owe the power to scorn them.
　　　　　　　　　　　　　　I despised
Men: from themselves I drew the pure ideal
By which to measure them.
　　　　　　　　　　　At woman's love
I laughed: but to that love I owe
The hunger for a more abiding love.
Their nestlings in our hearts leave vacant there

These hollow places, like a lark's round nest
Left empty in the grass, and filled with flowers.

What do I here alone? 'T was not so strange,
Weary of discords, that I chose to hear
The one, clear, perfect note of solitude;
But now it plagues the ear, that one shrill note:
Give me the chords back, even though some ring false.

Unmarried to the steel, the flint is cold:
Strike one to the other, and they wake in fire.

A solitary fagot will not burn:
Bring two, and cheerily the flame ascends.
Alone, man is a lifeless stone; or lies
A charring ember, smouldering into ash.

If the man riding yonder looks a speck,
The town an ant-hill, that is but the trick
Of our perspective: wisdom merely means
Correction of the angles at the eye.
I hold my hand up, so, before my face, —
It blots ten miles of country, and a town.
This little lying lens, that twists the rays,
So cheats the brain that My house, My affairs,
My hunger, or My happiness, My ache,
And My religion, fill immensity!

Yours merely dot the landscape casually.
'T is well God does not measure a man's worth
By the image on his neighbor's retina.

I am alone : the birds care not for me,
Except to sing a little farther off,
With looks that say, " What does this fellow here :
The loud brook babbles only for the flowers :
The mountain and the forest take me not
Into their meditations; I disturb
Their silence, as a child that drags his toy
Across a chapel's porch. The viewless ones
Who flattered me to claim their company
By gleams of thought they tossed to me for alms,
About their grander matters turn, nor deign
To notice me, unless it were to say —
As we put off a troublesome child — " There, go !
Men are your fellows, go and mate with them ! "

If I could find one soul that would not lie,
I would go back, and we would arm our hands,
And strike at every ugly weed that stands
　　In God's wide garden of the world, and try,
Obedient to the Gardener's commands,
　　To set some smallest flowers before we die.

　　One such I had found, —
But she was bound,

Fettered and led, bid for and sold,
Chained to a stone by a ring of gold.

In a stony sense the stone loved her, too :
Between our places the river was broad,
Should she tread on a broken heart to go through —
Could she put a man's life in mid-stream to be trod,
To come over dry-shod ?

Shame ! that a man with hand and brain
Should, like a love-lorn girl, complain,
Rhyming his dainty woes anew,
When there is honest work to do !

What work, what work ? Is God not wise
To rule the world He could devise ?
Yet see thou, though the realm be His,
He governs it by deputies.
Enough to know of Chance and Luck,
The stroke we choose to strike is struck ;
The deed we slight will slighted be,
In spite of all Necessity.
The Parcæ's web of good and ill
They weave with human shuttle still,
And fate is fate through man's free will.

With sullen thoughts that smoulder hour by hour,
In vague expectancy of help or hope

Which still eludes my brain, waiting I sit
Like a blind beggar at a palace-gate,
Who hears the rustling past of silks, and airs
Of costly odor mock him blowing by,
And feels within a dull and aching wish
That the proud wall would let some coping down
To crush him dead, and let him have his rest.

No help from men : they could not, if they would.
And God ? He lets His world be wrung with pain.
No help at all then ? Let life be in vain :
To get no help is surely greatest gain ;
To taunt the hunger down is sweetest food.

———————

O mocker, Memory ! From what floating cloud,
Or from what witchery of the haunted wood,
Or faintest perfumes, softly drifting through
The lupines' lattice-bars of white and blue,
Steals back upon my soul this weaker mood ?
My heart is dreaming ; — in a shadowy room
I breathe the vague scent of a jasmin-bloom
That floats on waves of music, softer played,
Till song and odor all the brain pervade ;
Swiftly across my cheek there sweeps the thrill
Of burning lips, — then all is hushed and still ;
And round the vision in unearthly awe
Deeps of enchanted starlight seem to draw,
In which my soul sinks, falling noiselessly —

As from a lone ship, far-off, in the night,
Out of a child's hand slips a pebble white,
Glimmering and fading down the awful sea.

———————

That night, which pushed me out of Paradise,
When the last guest had taken his mask of smiles
And gone, she wheeled a sofa from the light
Where I sat touching the piano-keys,
And begged me play her weariness away.
I played all sweet and solemn airs I knew,
And when, with music mesmerized, she slept,
I made the deep chords tell her dreams my love.
Once, when they grew too passionate, I saw
The faint blush ripen in their glow, and chide,
Even in dreams, the rash, tumultuous thought.
Then when I made them say, " Sleep on, dream on,
For now we are together; when thou wak'st
Forevermore we are alone — alone,"
She sighed in sleep, and waked not: then I rose,
And softly stooped my head, and, half in awe,
Half passion-rapt, I kissed her lips farewell.
—— Only the meek-mouthed blossoms kiss I now,
Or the cold cheek that sometimes comes at night
In haunted dreams, and brushes past my own.

Ah, what hast thou to do with me, sweet song —
Why hauntest thou and vexest so my dreams ?
Have I not turned away from thee so long —

So long, and yet the starry midnight seems
Astir with tremulous music, as of old, —
Forbidden memories opening, fold on fold?

O ghost of Love, why, with thy rose-leaf lips,
Dost thou still mock my sleep with kisses warm,
Torturing my dreams with touching finger tips,
That madden me to clasp thy phantom form?
Have I not earned, by all these tears, at last,
The right to rest untroubled by that Past?

Unto thy patient heart, my mother Earth,
I come, a weary child.
I have no claim, save that thou gav'st me birth,
And hast sustained me with thy nurture mild.
I have stood up alone these many years;
Now let me come and lie upon my face,
And spread my hands among the dewy grass,
Till the slow wind's mesmeric touches pass
Above my brain, and all its throbbing chase;
Into thy bosom take these bitter tears,
And let them seem unto the innocent flowers
Only as dew, or heaven's gentle showers;
Till, quieted and hushed against thy breast,
I can forget to weep,
And sink at last to sleep, —
Long sleep and rest.

Her face!
It must have been her face,—
No other one was ever half so fair,—
No other head e'er bent with such meek grace
Beneath that weight of beautiful blonde hair.
In a carriage on the street of the town,
Where I had strayed in walking from the bay,
Just as the sun was going down,
Shielding her sight from his latest ray,
She sat, and scanned with eager eye
The faces of the passers-by.
Whom was she looking for? Not me —
Yet what wild purpose can it be
That tempted her to this wild land?
— I marked that on her lifted hand
The diamonds no longer shine
Of the ring that meant, not mine — not mine!

Ah fool — fool — fool! crawl back to thy den,
Like a wounded beast as thou art, again;
Whosever she be, not thine — not thine!

I sat last night on yonder ridge of rocks
To see the sun set over Tamalpais,
Whose tented peak, suffused with rosy mist,
Blended the colors of the sea and sky
And made the mountain one great amethyst
Hanging against the sunset.

                              In the west
There lay two clouds which parted company,
Floating like two soft-breasted swans, and sailed
Farther and farther separate, till one stayed
To make a mantle for the evening-star;
The other wept itself away in rain.
A fancy seized me; — if, in other worlds,
That Spirit from afar should call to me!
Across some starry chasm impassable,
Weeping, " Oh, hadst thou only come to me! —
I loved you so! — I prayed each night that God
Would send you to me! Now, alas! too late,
Too late — farewell! " and still again, " farewell! "
Like the pulsation of a silenced bell
Whose sobs beat on within the brain.

                                      I rose,
And smote my staff strongly against the ground,
And set my face homeward, and set my heart
Firm in a passionate purpose : there, in haste,
With that one echo goading me to speed,
" If it should be too late — if it should be
Too late — too late! " I took a pen and wrote :

" Dear Soul, if I am mad to speak to thee,
And this faint glimmer which I call a hope
Be but the corpse-light on the grave of hope —
If thou, O darling Star, art in the West
To be my Evening-star, and watch my day

Fade slowly into desolate twilight, burn
This folly in the flames; and scattered with
Its ashes, let my madness be forgot.
But if not so, oh be my Morning-star,
And crown my East with splendor: come to me!"

   A stern, wild, broken place for a man to walk
And muse on broken fortunes; a rare place,—
There in the Autumn weather, cool and still,
With the warm sunshine clinging round the rocks
Softly, in pity, like a woman's love,—
To wait for some one who can never come
As a man there was waiting. Overhead
A happy bird sang quietly to himself,
Unconscious of such sombre thoughts below,
To which the song was background:—

                          "Yet how men
Sometimes will struggle, writhe, and scream at death!
It were so easy now, in the mild air,
To close the senses, slowly sleep, and die;
To cease to be the shaped and definite cloud,
And melt away into the fathomless blue;—
Only to touch this crimson thread of life,
Whose steady ripple pulses in my wrist,
And watch the little current soak the grass,
Till the haze came, then darkness, and then rest.
Would God be angry if I stopped one life

Among His myriads — such a worthless one ?
If I should pray, I wonder would He send
An angel down out of that great, white cloud,
(He surely could spare one from praising Him,)
To tell if there is any better way
Than — Look ! Why, that is grand, now ! (Am I
     mad ?
I did not think I should go mad !) That 's grand —
One of the blessed spirits come like this
To meet a poor, lean man among the rocks,
And answer questions for him ? "

                   There she stood,
With blonde hair blowing back, as if the breeze
Blew a light out of it, that ever played
And hovered at her shoulders. Such blue eyes
Mirrored the dreamy mountain distances, —
(Yet, are the angels' faces thin and wan
Like that ; and do they have such mouths, so drawn,
As if a sad song, some sad time, had died
Upon the lips, and left its echo there ?)

  And the man rose, and stood with folded hands
And head bent, and his downcast looks in awe
Touching her garment's hem, that, when she spoke,
Trembled a little where it met her feet.

  " I am come, because you called to me to come.
What were all other voices when I heard

The voice of my own soul's soul call to me?
You knew I loved you — oh, you must have known!
Was it a noble thing to do, you think,
To leave a lonely girl to die down there
In the great empty world, and come up here
To make a martyr's pillar of your pride?
There has been nobler work done, there in the world,
Than you have done this year!"

      Then cried the man:
" O voice that I have prayed for — O sad voice,
And woeful eyes, spare me if I have sinned!
There was a little ring you used to wear " —

" O strange, wild Fates, that balance bliss and woe
On such poor straws! It was a brother's gift."

" You never told me " —

      " Did you ever ask?"

" You, too, were surely prouder then than now!"

" Dear, I am sadder now: the head must bend
A little, when one 's weeping."

      Then the man, —
While half his mind, bewildered, at a flash
Took in the wide, lone place, the singing bird,
The sunshine streaming past them like a wind,

And the broad tree that moved as though it breathed:
" Oh, if 't is possible that in the world
There lies some low, mean work for me to do,
Let me go there alone : I am ashamed
To wear life's crown when I flung down its sword.
Crammed full of pride, and lust, and littleness,
O God, I am not worthy of thy gifts !
Let me find penance, till, years hence, perchance,
Made pure by toil, and scourged with pain and
        prayer " —

    Then a voice answered through His creature's lips,—
" God asks no penance but a better life.
He purifies by pain — He only ; 't is
A remedy too dangerous for our
Blind pharmacy. Lo ! we have tried that way,
And borne what fruit, or blossoms even, save one
Poor passion-flower ! Come, take thy happiness ;
In happy hearts are all the sunbeams forged
That brighten up our weatherbeaten world.
Come back with me — Come ! for I love you —
        Come ! "

    ———————

    If it was not a dream : perchance it was —
Often it seems so, and I wonder when
I shall awaken on the mountain-side,
With a little bitter taste left in the mouth
Of too much sleep, or too much happiness,
And sigh, and wish that I might dream again.

SUNDOWN

A SEA of splendor in the West,
  Purple, and pearl, and gold,
With milk-white ships of cloud, whose sails
  Slowly the winds unfold.

Brown cirrus-bars, like ribbed beach sand,
  Cross the blue upper dome;
And nearer flecks of feathery white
  Blow over them like foam.

But when that transient glory dies
  Into the twilight gray,
And leaves me on the beach alone
  Beside the glimmering bay;

And when I know that, late or soon,
  Love's glory finds a grave,
And hearts that danced like dancing foam
  Break like the breaking wave;

A little dreary, homeless thought
  Creeps sadly over me,
Like the shadow of a lonely cloud
  Moving along the sea.

THE ARCH

JUST where the street of the village ends,
  Over the road an oak-tree tall,
Curving in more than a crescent, bends
  With an arch like the gate of a Moorish wall.

Over across the river there,
  Looking under the arch, one sees
The sunshine slant through the distant air,
  And burn on the cliff and the tufted trees.

Each day, hurrying through the town,
  I stop an instant, early or late,
As I cross the street, and glancing down
  I catch a glimpse through the Moorish gate.

Only a moment there I stand,
  But I look through that loop in the dusty air,
Into a far-off fairyland,
  Where all seems calm, and kind, and fair.

So sometimes at the end of a thought,
  Where with a vexing doubt we 've striven,
A sudden, sunny glimpse is caught
  Of an open arch, and a peaceful heaven.

APRIL IN OAKLAND

Was there last night a snowstorm?
  So thick the orchards stand,
With drift on drift of blossom-flakes
  Whitening all the land.

Or have the waves of life that swelled
  The green buds, day by day,
Broken at once in clinging foam
  And scattered odor-spray?

The winds come drowsy with the breath
  Of cherry and of pear,
Sighing their perfume-laden wings
  No more of sweet can bear.

Over the garden-gateway
  That parts the tufted hedge,
Rimming the idly twinkling bay,
  Sleeps the blue mountains' edge.

Yon fleece of clouds in heaven,
  So delicate and fair,
Seems a whole league of orchard-bloom
  Sailing along the air.

Oh, loveliness of nature!
  Oh, sordid minds of men!
Without, a world of bloom and balm —
  A sour, sad soul within.

O winds that sweep the orchard
  With Orient spices sweet,
Why bring ye with that desolate sound
  The dead leaves to my feet?

Ah, sweeter were the fragrance
  That I to-day have found,
If last year's crumbled leaves of love
  Were buried under ground;

And fairer were the shadowed troops
  That fleck the distant hill,
If shades of clouds that will not pass
  Dimmed not my memory still.

Better than all the beauty
  Which cloud or blossom shows
Is the blue sky that arches all
  With measureless repose.

And better than the bright blue sky,
  To know that far away
Sweep all the silent host of stars
  Behind the veil of day.

And best to feel that there and here,
    About us and above,
Move on the purposes of God
    In justice and in love.

TO CHILD SARA

I LOOKED in a dew-drop's heart to-day
    As it clung on a leaf of clover,
Holding a sparkle of starry light,
Like a liquid drop of opal bright
    With diamond dusted over.

In that least globe of quivering dew
    The sunny scene around,
Diminished to a grass-blade's width —
Scarcely a fairy's finger-breadth
    All imaged there I found:

The spreading oak, the fir's soft fringe,
    The grain-field's brightening green,
The linnet that flew fluttering by,
And, over all, the dear blue sky,
    The bending boughs between:

And all the night, as from its nest
    It gazes up afar,
Its bosom holds the heavens deep,
Whose constellations o'er it sweep,
    And mirrors every star.

Child, is that drop of dew — your soul —
   With mirrored heaven as bright?
(Forgive me that I ask of you,
Whose heart I know is pure and true
   And stainless as the light):

The sunshine, and the starlight too, —
   Fair hope, and faith as fair,
Courage, and patience, silent power,
And wisdom for each troubled hour, —
   Tell me, are they all there?

Your quiet grace and kindly words
   Have influence sweet and strong;
Your hand and voice can calm the brain
And cheer the heavy hearts of men
   With music and with song:

Let the soul answer — can it give
   That music clear and calm —
The rhythmic years, the holier aim,
The scorn of pleasure, fortune, fame —
   To make our life a psalm?

All round the house, your birthday morn
   The budded orchards stand;
And we can watch from every room
The trees all blushing into bloom —
   Blossoms on every hand:

So may your Life be, many a year,
    A fair and goodly tree;
Not blossoming only, but sublime
With fruit, so hastening the time
    When Earth shall Eden be.

EASTERN WINTER

Cold — cold — the very sun looks cold,
With those thin rays of chilly gold
Laid on that gap of bluish sky
That glazes like a dying eye.

The naked trees are shivering,
Each cramped and bare branch quivering,
Cutting the bleak wind into blades,
Whose edge to brain and bone invades.

That hard ground seems to ache, all day,
Even for a sheet of snow, to lay
Upon its icy feet and knees,
Stretched stiffly there to freeze and freeze.

And yon shrunk mortal — what's within
That nipped and winter-shriveled skin?
The pinched face drawn in peevish lines,
The voice that through his blue lips whines, —

The frost has got within, you see, —
Left but a selfish *me* and *me* :
The heart is chilled, its nerves are numb,
And love has long been frozen dumb.

Ah, give me back the clime I know,
Where all the year geraniums blow,
And hyacinth-buds bloom white for snow;

Where hearts beat warm with life's delight,
Through radiant winter's sunshine bright,
And summer's starry deeps of night;

Where man may let earth's beauty thaw
The wintry creed which Calvin saw,
That God is only Power and Law;

And out of Nature's Bible prove,
That here below as there above
Our Maker — Father — God — is Love.

SLEEPING

HUSHED within her quiet bed
    She is lying all the night,
    In her pallid robes of white,
    Eyelids on the pure eyes pressed,
    Soft hands folded on the breast, —
And you thought I meant it — dead?

Nay! I smile at your shocked face:
    In the morning she will wake,
    Turn her dreams to sport, and make
    All the household glad and gay,
    Yet for many a merry day,
With her beauty and her grace.

But some summer 't will be said, —
    " She is lying all the night,
    In her pallid robes of white,
    Eyelids on the tired eyes pressed,
    Hands that cross upon the breast: "
We shall understand it — dead!

Yet 't will only be a sleep:
    When, with songs and dewy light,
    Morning blossoms out of night,
    She will open her blue eyes
    'Neath the palms of Paradise,
While we foolish ones shall weep.

STARLIGHT

THEY think me daft, who nightly meet
My face turned starward, while my feet
Stumble along the unseen street;

But should man's thoughts have only room
For Earth, his cradle and his tomb,
Not for his Temple's grander gloom?

And must the prisoner all his days
Learn but his dungeon's narrow ways
And never through its grating gaze?

Then let me linger in your sight,
My only amaranths! blossoming bright
As over Eden's cloudless night.

The same vast belt, and square, and crown,
That on the Deluge glittered down,
And lit the roofs of Bethlehem town!

Ye make me one with all my race,
A victor over time and space,
Till all the path of men I pace.

Far-speeding backward in my brain
We build the Pyramids again,
And Babel rises from the plain ;

And climbing upward on your beams
I peer within the Patriarchs' dreams,
Till the deep sky with angels teems.

My Comforters ! — Yea, why not mine ?
The power that kindled you doth shine,
In man, a mastery divine ;

That Love which throbs in every star,
And quickens all the worlds afar,
Beats warmer where his children are.

The shadow of the wings of Death
Broods over us ; we feel his breath :
" Resurgam " still the spirit saith.

These tired feet, this weary brain,
Blotted with many a mortal stain,
May crumble earthward — not in vain.

With swifter feet that shall not tire,
Eyes that shall fail not at your fire
Nearer your splendors I aspire.

A DEAD BIRD IN WINTER

The cold, hard sky and hidden sun,
  The stiffened trees that shiver so,
With bare twigs naked every one
  To these harsh winds that freeze the snow, —

It was a bitter place to die,
  Poor birdie! Was it easier, then,
On such a world to shut thine eye,
  And sleep away from life, than when

The apple-blossoms tint the air,
  And, twittering in the sunny trees,
Thy fellow-songsters flit and pair,
  Breasting the warm, caressing breeze?

Nay, it were easiest, I feel,
  Though 't were a brighter Earth to lose,
To let the summer shadows steal
  About thee, bringing their repose;

When the noon hush was on the air,
  And on the flowers the warm sun shined,
And Earth seemed all so sweet and fair,
  That He who made it must be kind.

So I, too, could not bear to go
  From Life in this unfriendly clime,
To lie beneath the crusted snow,
  When the dead grass stands stiff with rime;

But under those blue skies of home,
  Far easier were it to lie down
Where the perpetual violets bloom
  And the rich moss grows never brown;

Where linnets never cease to build
  Their nests, in boughs that always wave
To odorous airs, with blessing filled
  From nestled blossoms round my grave.

SPRING TWILIGHT

SINGING in the rain, robin?
  Rippling out so fast
All thy flute-like notes, as if
  This singing were thy last!

After sundown, too, robin?
  Though the fields are dim,
And the trees grow dark and still,
  Dripping from leaf and limb.

'T is heart-broken music, —
  That sweet, faltering strain, —
Like a mingled memory,
  Half ecstasy, half pain.

Surely thus to sing, robin,
  Thou must have in sight
Beautiful skies behind the shower,
  And dawn beyond the night.

Would thy faith were mine, robin!
  Then, though night were long,
All its silent hours should melt
  Their sorrow into song.

EVENING

THE Sun is gone: those glorious chariot-wheels
Have sunk their broadening spokes of flame, and left
Thin rosy films wimpled across the West,
Whose last faint tints melt slowly in the blue,
As the last trembling cadence of a song
Fades into silence sweeter than all sound.

Now the first stars begin to tremble forth
Like the first instruments of an orchestra
Touched softly, one by one. —— There in the East
Kindles the glory of moonrise: how its waves
Break in a surf of silver on the clouds! ——
White, motionless clouds, like soft and snowy wings
Which the great Earth spreads, sailing round the Sun.

O silent stars! that over ages past
Have shone serenely as ye shine to-night,
Unseal, unseal the secret that ye keep!
Is it not time to tell us why we live?
Through all these shadowy corridors of years
(Like some gray Priest, who through the Mysteries
Led the blindfolded Neophyte in fear),
Time leads us blindly onward, till in wrath
Tired Life would seize and throttle its stern guide,

And force him tell us *whither* and *how long*.
But Time gives back no answer — only points
With motionless finger to eternity,
Which deepens over us, as that deep sky
Darkens above me : only its vestibule
Glimmers with scattered stars ; and down the West
A silent meteor slowly slides afar,
As though, pacing the garden-walks of heaven,
Some musing seraph had let fall a flower.

THE ORGAN

It is no harmony of human making,
  Though men have built those pipes of burnished
      gold;
Their music, out of Nature's heart awaking,
  Forever new, forever is of old.

Man makes not — only finds — all earthly beauty,
  Catching a thread of sunshine here and there,
Some shining pebble in the path of duty,
  Some echo of the songs that flood the air.

That prelude is a wind among the willows,
  Rising until it meets the torrent's roar;
Now a wild ocean, beating his great billows
  Among the hollow caverns of the shore.

It is the voice of some vast people, pleading
  For justice from an ancient shame and wrong, —
The tramp of God's avenging armies, treading
  With shouted thunders of triumphant song.

O soul, that sittest chanting dreary dirges,
  Couldst thou but rise on some divine desire,

As those deep chords upon their swelling surges
　　Bear up the wavering voices of the choir!

But ever lurking in the heart, there lingers
　　The trouble of a false and jarring tone,
As some great Organ which unskillful fingers
　　Vex into discords when the Master's gone.

LOST LOVE

Bury it, and sift
   Dust upon its light, —
Death must not be left,
   To offend the sight.

Cover the old love —
   Weep not on the mound —
Grass shall grow above,
   Lilies spring around.

Can we fight the law,
   Can our natures change —
Half-way through withdraw —
   Other lives exchange ?

You and I must do
   As the world has done,
There is nothing new
   Underneath the sun.

Fill the grave up full —
   Put the dead love by —
Not that men are dull,
   Not that women lie, —

But 't is well and right —
Safest, you will find —
That the Out of Sight
Should be Out of Mind

A MEMORY

Upon the barren, lonely hill
  We sat to watch the sinking sun;
Below, the land grew dim and still,
  Whose evening shadow had begun.
Her finger parted the shut book, —
  At " Aylmer's Field " the leaf was turned, —
Round her meek head and sainted look
  The sunset like a halo burned.
She knew not that I watched her face —
  Her spirit through her eyes was gone
To some far-off and Sabbath place,
  And left me gazing there alone.
Could she have known, that quiet hour,
  What ghosts her presence raised in me,
What graves were opened by the power
  Of that unconscious witchery,
She would not thus have sat and seen
  The bird that balanced far below
On the blue air, and watched the sheen
  Along his broad wings come and go.
For was she not another's bride?
  And I — what right had I to feast
Upon those eyes in revery wide,
  With hungering gaze like famished beast?

Was it before my fate I knelt —
    The human fate, the mighty law —
To hunger for the heart I felt,
    And love the lovely face I saw ?
Or was it only that the brow,
    Or some sweet trick of hand or tone,
Brought from the Past to haunt me now
    Her ghost whose love was mine alone ?
I know not; but we went to rest
    That eve, from songs that haunt me still,
And all night long, in visions blest,
    I walked with angels on the hill.

LIFE

Forenoon and afternoon and night, — Forenoon,
And afternoon, and night, — Forenoon, and — what!
The empty song repeats itself. No more?
Yea, that is Life: make this forenoon sublime,
This afternoon a psalm, this night a prayer,
And Time is conquered, and thy crown is won.

FERTILITY

CLEAR water on smooth rock
Could give no foothold for a single flower,
Or slenderest shaft of grain :
The stone must crumble under storm and rain,
The forests crash beneath the whirlwind's power,
And broken boughs from many a tempest-shock,
And fallen leaves of many a wintry hour,
Must mingle in the mould,
Before the harvest whitens on the plain,
Bearing an hundred-fold.
Patience, O weary heart !
Let all thy sparkling hours depart,
And all thy hopes be withered with the frost,
And every effort tempest-tost —
So, when all life's green leaves
Are fallen, and mouldered underneath the sod,
Thou shalt go not too lightly to thy God,
But heavy with full sheaves.

THREE SONGS

Sing me, thou Singer, a song of gold!
    Said a careworn man to me:
So I sang of the golden summer days,
And the sad, sweet autumn's yellow haze,
Till his heart grew soft, and his mellowed gaze
    Was a kindly sight to see.

Sing me, dear Singer, a song of love!
    A fair girl asked of me:
Then I sang of a love that clasps the Race,
Gives all, asks naught — till her kindled face
Was radiant with the starry grace
    Of blessed Charity.

Sing me, O Singer, a song of life!
    Cried an eager youth to me:
And I sang of the life without alloy,
Beyond our years, till the heart of the boy
Caught the golden beauty, and love, and joy
    Of the great Eternity.

THE WORLD'S SECRET

I KNOW the splendor of the Sun,
  And beauty in the leaves, and moss, and grass;
I love the birds' small voices every one,
  And all the hours have kindness as they pass;

But still the heart can apprehend
  A deeper purport than the brain may know:
I see it at the dying daylight's end,
  And hear it when the winds begin to blow.

It strives to speak from all the world,
  Out of dumb earth, and moaning ocean-tides;
And brooding Night, beneath her pinions furled,
  Some message writ in starry cipher hides.

Must I go seeking everywhere
  The meanings that behind our objects be —
A depth serener in the azure air,
  A something more than peace upon the sea?

Not one least deed one soul to bless?
  Unto the stern-eyed Future shall I bear
Only the sense of pain without redress,
  Self-sickness, and a dull and stale despair?

Nay, let me shape, in patience slow,
  My years, like the Holy Child his bird of clay,
Till suddenly the clod its Master know,
  And thrill with life, and soar with songs away.

SEEMING AND BEING

THE brave old motto, " Seem not — only be," —
Would it were set ablaze against the sky
In golden letters, where the world must read !
What is there done for the honest doing's sake,
In these poor times gone mad with self-parade ?
There 's not a picture of the Cross but bears
The painter's name as prominent as the Christ's :
There 's not a scene, of such peculiar grace
That one would fain forget men's meanness there,
But from the rocks some rascal clothier's name
Stares in great capitals, till one could wish
The knave hung from his signboard, for a sign :
There 's not a graveyard in the land, but lo !
On the white tablets of the dead, full cut
Below their sacred names, his shameless name
Who carved the marble !

                Is it not pitiful ?
We are all actors, and all audience.
Yea, such a dreary farce we make our lives,
That something is expected of a man
Upon his deathbed : " Hark ye now, good friends,
These fine last words, this notable bravery, — see ! "
So even the grim cross-bones of awful Death

Must take an attitude, and the skull smirk
For a last picture.

         Here is a nation, too
(God help it!), that dare scarcely act its mind,
But walks the world's stage, quaking with the thought,
"What will great England think of me for this?"

The poet scoffs at fame, then sets himself,
Full-titled, with a portrait at the front;
Each beautiful impatient soul who left
The world he scorned, still lingered near enough
To listen, not displeased, and hear the world
Admiringly relate how he had scorned it;
Even our great doubting Thomas, in young days
When he praised silence, did it with loud speech,
That ever too distinctly told, "'T is I,
Thomas, so noisily abuse your noise!"

Is it not enough for the trumpet that the god
Has chosen it to sound his message through?
Must the brass blare in its own petty praise?
And can we never do the right, and do it
As though we were alone upon the earth,
And the gods blind?

WEATHER-BOUND

Thou pitiless, false sea!
How, like a woman, thou wilt softly sigh
  With heaving breast where bubble-jewels shine,
Or, beckoning, toss thy foam-white arms on high,
  And laugh with those blue sunny eyes of thine!

Ah, crouching, creeping sea!
Thou tiger-cat! how, while the winds make pause
  To stroke thy long smooth back in quiet play,
Thou canst unsheathe thy velvet-hidden claws
  And spring all unawares upon thy prey!

Thou treacherous, cruel sea!
How thou wilt show thy glittering smile at night,
  Hiding thy fangs, hushing thy fiendish cry,
And rise all gentle sport from licking white
  The bones of men that underneath thee lie!

O bitter, bitter sea!
Didst thou not fawn about my naked feet,
  When I stood with thee on the beach, and say
That thou wouldst bear me swiftly home to meet
  My darling, waiting there in vain to-day?

Yea, thou most mighty sea!
Keep then that promise murmured on the shore;
    Put thy great shoulders to our loitering keel,
Not as in rage and wrath thou hast before —
    Let the good ship thy help gigantic feel.

Thou answerest me, O sea!
Lifting in silence, o'er the waters stilled,
    The shattered fragment of a rainbow fair,
A mocking promise, ne'er to be fulfilled,
    Based on the waves and broken in mid-air.

SUMMER AFTERNOON

Far in hollow mountain cañons
Brood with purple-folded pinions,
Flocks of drowsy distance-colors on their nests;
And the bare round slopes for forests
Have cloud-shadows, floating forests,
On their breasts.

Winds are wakening and dying,
Questions low with low replying,
Through the oak a hushed and trembling whisper
goes:
Faint and rich the air with odors,
Hyacinth and spicy odors
Of the rose.

Even the flowerless acacia
Is one flower — such slender stature,
With its latticed leaves a-tremble in the sun:
They have shower-drops for blossoms,
Quivering globes of diamond blossoms,
Every one.

In the blue of heaven holy
Clouds go floating, floating slowly,

Pure in snowy robe and sunny silver crown ;
   And they seem like gentle angels —
   Leisure-full and loitering angels,
         Looking down.

   Half the birds are wild with singing,
   And the rest with rhythmic winging
Sing in melody of motion to the sight ;
   Every little sparrow twitters,
   Cheerily chirps, and cheeps, and twitters
         His delight.

   Sad at heart amid the splendor,
   Dull to all the radiance tender,
What can I for such a world give back again ?
   Could I only hint the beauty —
   Some least shadow of the beauty,
         Unto men !

A POET'S APOLOGY

TRUTH cut on high in tablets of hewn stone,
　Or on great columns gorgeously adorned,
Perchance were left alone,
　Passed by and scorned;
But Truth enchased upon a jewel rare,
A man would keep, and next his bosom wear.

So, many an hour, I sit and carve my gems —
　Ten spoiled, for one in purer beauty set:
Not for kings' diadems —
　Some amulet
That may be worn o'er hearts that toil and plod, —
Though but one pearl that bears the name of God.

A PRAYER

O God, our Father, if we had but truth!
   Lost truth — which thou perchance
Didst let man lose, lest all his wayward youth
   He waste in song and dance;
That he might gain, in searching, mightier powers
For manlier use in those foreshadowed hours.

If, blindly groping, he shall oft mistake,
   And follow twinkling motes
Thinking them stars, and the one voice forsake
   Of Wisdom for the notes
Which mocking Beauty utters here and there,
Thou surely wilt forgive him, and forbear!

Oh, love us, for we love thee, Maker — God!
   And would creep near thy hand,
And call thee " Father, Father," from the sod
   Where by our graves we stand,
And pray to touch, fearless of scorn or blame,
Thy garment's hem, which Truth and Good we name.

A DAILY MIRACLE

June's sunshine on the broad porch shines
Through tangled curtains of crossing vines;
The restless dancing of the leaves
Dusky webs of shadow weaves,
That wander on the oaken floor,
Or cross the threshold of the door.
Scattered where'er their mazes run
Lie little phantoms of the sun:
Whatever chink the sunbeam found,
Crooked or narrow, on the ground
The shadowy image still is round.

So the image of God in the heart of a man,
Which truth makes, rifting as it can
Through the narrow crooked ways
Of our restless deeds and days,
Still is His image — bright or dim —
And scorning it is scorning Him.

INFLUENCES

From the scarlet sea of sunset,
  Tossing up its waves of fire
To a floating spray of splendor,
  Kindles through me mad desire
    Now — now — now to call her mine!

From the ashen gray of twilight
  Musings dark as shadows linger,
Slowly creeping, leave me weeping —
  While in silence round my finger
    That long glossy lock I twine.

From the holy hush of starlight
  Sinks a peace upon my spirit,
And a voice of hope and patience —
  All the quiet night I hear it —
    Whispers, " Wait, for she is thine!"

POEMS WRITTEN BETWEEN 1867 AND 1872

A BIRD'S SONG

THE shadow of a bird
  On the shadow of a bough;
Sweet and clear his song is heard,
   "Seek me now — I seek thee now."
The bird swings out of reach in the swaying tree,
But his shadow on the garden walk below belongs to
      me.

The phantom of my Love
  False dreams with hope doth fill,
Softly singing far above,
   "Love me still — I love thee still!"
The cruel vision hovers at my sad heart's door,
But the soul-love is soaring out of reach forevermore.

THE NEWS-GIRL

A TINY, blue-eyed, elfin lass
Meets me upon the street I pass
   In going to the ferry;
Barefooted, scantly clothed, and thin,
With little weazen cheeks and chin,
   Yet always chirk and merry:
   Ever merry, however pale,
I always hear her, as I draw near her:
   " 'Ere 's the Mail, sir! — Mail? — Mail?"

With that same piping little tune,
She waits there every afternoon,
   Selling her bunch of papers;
She scarcely looks aside to see
What 's passing by, of grief or glee —
   No childish tricks or capers;
   Her pattering bare feet never fail
To run and meet me, and chirping greet me,
   " 'Ere 's the Mail, sir! — Mail? — Mail?"

Her dingy frock is scant and torn;
Her old, old face looks wan and worn,
   Yet always sweet and sunny;
Week in, week out, she is the same —

I asked her once what was her name,
   And, jingling all her money,
   Holding a paper up for sale,
The little midget answered, " Bridget !
    Want the Mail, sir ? — Mail ? — Mail ? "

I wonder where she goes at night,
And in what nook the poor young sprite
   Finds room for rest and sleeping ;
I wonder if her little bones
Go home to blows and cuffs, and tones
   That roughly set her weeping —
   When, rainy days, the pennies fail
And few are buying, for all her crying,
    " 'Ere 's the Mail, sir ! — Mail ? — Mail ? "

O rich and happy people ! you
Whose ways are smooth, and woes are few,
   Whose life brims o'er with blisses,
Pity the little patient face,
That never knows the tender grace
   Of kind caress or kisses.
   For you, the blessings never fail ;
For her 't is only to wait there lonely
    And cry, " The Mail, sir ? — Mail ? —Mail ? "

THE HOUSE AND THE HEART

EVERY house with its garret,
Lumbered with rubbish and relics, —
Spinning-wheels leaning in corners,
Chests under spider-webbed rafters,
Brittle and yellow old letters,
Grandfather's things and grandmother's.
There overhead, at the midnight,
Noises of creaking and stepping
Startle the hush of the chambers —
Ghosts on their tiptoes repassing.

Every house with its garden;
Some little plot — a half-acre,
Or a mere strip by the windows,
Flower-beds and narrow box-borders,
Something spicily fragrant,
Something azure and golden.
There the small feet of the sparrow
Star the fresh mould round the roses;
And, in the shadowy moonlight,
Wonderful secrets are whispered.

Every heart with its garret,
Cumbered with relics and rubbish —
Wheels that are silent forever,
Leaves that are faded and broken,

Foolish old wishes and fancies,
Cobwebs of doubt and suspicion —
Useless, unbeautiful, growing
Year by year thicker and faster :
Naught but a fire or a moving
Ever can clear it, or clean it.

Every heart with its garden ;
Some little corner kept sacred,
Fragrant and pleasant with blossoms ;
There the forget-me-nots cluster,
And pure love-violets, hidden,
Guessed but by sweetness all round them ;
Some little strip in the sunshine,
Cheery and warm, for above it
Rest the deep, beautiful heavens,
Blue, and beyond, and forever.

A PRAYER FOR PEACE

FATHER in Heaven! humbly before thee
   Kneeling in prayer thy children appear;
We in our weakness, we in our blindness,
   Thou in thy wisdom, hear us, oh hear!

God watching o'er us sleeps not nor slumbers,
   Faithful night watches his angels keep.
Through all the darkness, unto the dawning,
   To his beloved he giveth sleep.

A TROPICAL MORNING AT SEA

Sky in its lucent splendor lifted
  Higher than cloud can be;
Air with no breath of earth to stain it,
  Pure on the perfect sea.

Crests that touch and tilt each other,
  Jostling as they comb;
Delicate crash of tinkling water,
  Broken in pearling foam.

Plashings — or is it the pinewood's whispers,
  Babble of brooks unseen,
Laughter of winds when they find the blossoms,
  Brushing aside the green?

Waves that dip, and dash, and sparkle;
  Foam-wreaths slipping by,
Soft as a snow of broken roses
  Afloat over mirrored sky.

Off to the East the steady sun-track
  Golden meshes fill —
Webs of fire, that lace and tangle,
  Never a moment still.

Liquid palms but clap together,
  Fountains, flower-like, grow —
Limpid bells on stems of silver —
  Out of a slope of snow.

Sea-depths, blue as the blue of violets —
  Blue as a summer sky,
When you blink at its arch sprung over
  Where in the grass you lie.

Dimly an orange bit of rainbow
  Burns where the low west clears,
Broken in air, like a passionate promise
  Born of a moment's tears.

Thinned to amber, rimmed with silver,
  Clouds in the distance dwell,
Clouds that are cool, for all their color,
  Pure as a rose-lipped shell.

Fleets of wool in the upper heavens
  Gossamer wings unfurl;
Sailing so high they seem but sleeping
  Over yon bar of pearl.

What would the great world lose, I wonder —
  Would it be missed or no —
If we stayed in the opal morning,
  Floating forever so?

Swung to sleep by the swaying water,
    Only to dream all day —
Blow, salt wind from the north upstarting,
    Scatter such dreams away !

THE PICTURE OF THE WORLD

ONE morning of a summer's day,
Upon a painter's easel lay
The picture of a child at play :
A form of laughing life and grace,
And finished all except the place
Left empty for the untouched face.
In nodding violets, half asleep,
The dancing feet were ankle deep :
One rounded arm was heaping up
With clover-bloom and buttercup;
The other tossed a blossom high
To lure a wandering butterfly.
   'T was easy to imagine there
In that round frame of rippling hair
The wanting face, all bright and fair.

A sadder artist came that day,
Looked at the picture where it lay,
And, sitting in the painter's place,
He painted in the missing face.
From his own heart the lines he took —
Lo! what a wan and woeful look!
Under the mocking wreath of flowers,
A brow worn old with weary hours :

A face, once seen, one still must see;
Wise, awful-eyed solemnity,
Lips long ago too tired to hide
The torture-lines where love had died;
The look of a despair too late,
Too dead even to be desperate;
A face for which so far away
The struggle and the protest lay,
No memory of it more could stay.
Repulsed and reckless, withered, wild,
It stared above the dancing child.

At night a musing poet came
And, shuddering, wrote beneath its name.

FOR THE GIFTS OF THE SPIRIT

SEND down thy truth, O God!
Too long the shadows frown;
Too long the darkened way we 've trod:
Thy truth, O Lord, send down!

Send down thy Spirit free,
Till wilderness and town
One temple for thy worship be:
Thy Spirit, oh, send down!

Send down thy love, thy life,
Our lesser lives to crown,
And cleanse them of their hate and strife:
Thy living love send down!

Send down thy peace, O Lord!
Earth's bitter voices drown
In one deep ocean of accord:
Thy peace, O God, send down!

THE TWO WAYS

'T was Sabbath; and, with clang on clang,
A deafening crash of church bells rang:
The day for penance and for dole,
For sackcloth and an ashen soul —
So had my childhood learned in fear.
And forth I fared, with mood severe,
Clad in my soberest and best,
With God's own world to keep his Rest.
Through orchard, field, and wood I paced,
Rasping a dry thought, solemn-faced.
But suddenly, "What is this?" I thought;
"Does Earth keep Sabbath as she ought?"
And looking round about, I sought
Some comrade with me, on my way,
In woeful weeds to drape the day.
— All nature given o'er to glee!
No psalms, no dirge, no minor key;
Each grass-blade nodding to the rest,
As one who knows a hidden jest;
The thrush still hurrying, loud and gay,
To find the lost thread of his lay;
And chasing, as he flies along,
The fleeing ripple of his song,
The giddy bluebird flits and sings —

A bit of azure sky on wings.
Down the tree-trunks the shadows trace
The tremble of their dancing lace;
The drifting apple-blossoms meek
Brush their white kisses by my cheek;
The bobolink bubbles o'er with glee
In tumbling, headlong melody;
And from the catbird's hedge is sent
His quick, low chuckle of content.

In all that choral symphony
Of flower, and bird, and waving tree,
And happy sky, and laughing sun,
I found in holy woe not one.
— Save only, through the churchyard gloom
Returning, at a new-made tomb
A bitter mourner, black-arrayed,
Whom fools in robes had faithless made,
Wept the lost angel he had wed
As though her soul — and God — were dead.
Him only; and, as evening fell,
An owl, that sought some mate as well,
Was hooting from his hollow tree —
" Will none be doleful now with me,
Will none with me sad penance do ? "
And still he hooted: " Who ? — who, who ? "

THE CLOCKS OF GNOSTER-TOWN

IT was ever so many years ago,
In the days when few were wise, and so
All thought they were wiser than any, you know,
In the kingdom of Mhundus over the sea,
The town of Gnoster used to be;
And on a day which is known to me
Yunus, a small man, bald and brown,
Came to dwell in this Gnoster-town.

'T was a queer little village, getting full
Already when Yunus arrived; quite dull,
Or a little stupid, you might say,
For the Now was ruled by the Yesterday,
And highly indecorous it was deemed
To differ from what one's neighbors seemed,
So the average ran rather low,
Respectable though, as majorities go,
And the social tone was safe, but slow.

All over Mhundus time was law;
'T was the promptest kingdom ever you saw,
The royal rule was, " Follow the sun;
Do what you do when 't is time 't was done.
Do with your might; seek wisdom, pursue it;
Don't wait for the licensed venders to do it."

So Gnoster, too, went in for time

In its feeble way, and thought the chime
Of its thousand clocks pealed out so far
That they kept the hour for the furtherest star;
And many a citizen demure
Slept sound and sweet, in the thought secure
That Caph and Phad could scarce go wrong
While Gnoster clocks beat staunch and strong.

A thousand clocks! But for setting them going
The village a terrible tax was owing.
Not to mention the cost and care
Of keeping them all in good repair;
For the clock-tinker's trade, all up and down,
Was one of the very best in town.

There was the clock on the great town-hall,
Frowning over its spike-toothed wall.
It made the base for a liberty-pole,
Whose crest meant, Everybody had stole
Somebody's cap, and gilded it so
That the owner never his own could know.
Hugging the dial with bent arm bone
Sat a figure of Justice, asleep in stone;
Her broken sword had been crooked, at best;
In one of her scales was a hornet's nest;
And the bandage over her stony eyes,
What with the weather, and what with the flies,
A pair of gold spectacles you would think,
With one eye screwed in a pleasant wink.

There was the clock at the factory yard,
Ticking and clicking sharp and hard,

With a dingy little iron face,
And a bell that banged the hours apace.
The dial was flat, the figures were lean
As if half-starved — all cheap and mean ;
And a timid flower, in a chink forlorn,
The hands had scissored and dropped in scorn.

    On an ancient, somewhat ruined building
Was a college clock ; no paint or gilding,
Stern and classic, dreary and dread,
And the ivy on it was dead — all dead.
Some cherubs were sculptured around in places,
But the moss was growing on their faces,
And the dial was propped by an angel which
Had been clipped in the wings to fit its niche.
In the old stone belfry's chinks and loops,
With coo and flutter the soft white troops
Of the doves were just beginning to come,
With a breath of purity and home.

    Hundreds such secular ones he saw,
But the great church clocks laid down the law.
Throned on the stone cathedral's tower,
A huge old time-piece thundered the hour.
Its face like a face in a mask appeared,
For above, it scowled, and below, it leered.
The dial figures were shrunken men,
And Peter's keys made the X for ten.
The hour-hand clawed as an invitation
Beckoning every tribe and nation,
But a trick of perspective made you suppose

The finger was laid aside of the nose.
The wheels all creaked and groaned as they went;
It would soon run down, that was evident.
  Close on the great cathedral's toes
A spick-span little building rose,
With a door like the arch of a Roman nose.
Its Gothic windows were stained so thick
That scant was the light that could through them prick.
Around on the spires were a dozen clocks,
As though they had settled there in flocks —
A brood from its neighbor's single tower;
And whenever the old clock struck the hour,
These little gilt ones with all their power
Chimed hurriedly in. They were all so made
That lively Italian tunes they played,
And odd little figures, all arrayed
In patch-work petticoats, trotted out
(Moved by machinery, no doubt),
And bobbed, and trotted in again,
Every time that the hands said when.
In place of Peter's keys for ten
Was a fat St. Timothy, going to take
A little wine for his stomach's sake.
  Up a street that was always choked with people
Was a great, thick clock, on a great, thick steeple.
'T was a wooden building, big and bare,
With not much light, but plenty of air,
And a dead-earnest look, as if the man
That made it had understood his plan.

'T was a thumping, whacking clock, that would chase
All sensitive birds away from the place,
And it seemed to have struck itself red in the face.

   One clock, on a building of colors various,
Had beside it a statue of St. Arius.
The dial-face seemed made of shell,
It shifted its changeable hues so well.
Its figure three had been whittled away,
And it wore a smile which seemed to say
That all was sweet and nothing vile,
And the universe made of sugar and style;
That this hitherto troublesome mortal coil
Could be made quite smooth with honey and oil.
'T was really a little hard to say,
In spite of its air of being *au fait*,
Exactly what was its time of day;
Its pointers were stretched so far from the dial,
That you gave it up, on the second trial,
For you saw at once it depended rather
Which side you stood, and how near it, whether
The hand and a figure fell together.

   But a positive clock, on a new French school,
Seemed to pride itself it was no such fool
To go groping around to follow the sun :
Why, who could prove there *was* any sun ?
So its hands were nailed at half-past one,
And its wheels, all dust, in a crust of rust,
Were bound not to budge till 't was proved they
     must.

Well, besides these and hundreds more,
Each man had a watch, and over his door
A family clock, and folks do say
That many a soul kept hidden away
In a secret pocket, innerly sewed,
A private watch that he never showed,
Which the maker and giver had begged might be
Kept with the great sun to agree.
But nobody trusted to these — not one.
It was too much trouble to take the sun,
And, besides, it would bring on knocks and shocks
From the public to differ with the clocks.
So by them they ate, drank, rose, and slept,
Blessed and cursed, rejoiced and wept.

And every clock thought: "Ho! my chime
Keeps the great world in tune and time!"
And every church thought: "Ho! my tower
Points upward, motionless, hour by hour —
Aims ever the same with steadfast power!"
And little they knew, as they watched the blue,
That round with the plump old earth they flew,
Eternally shifting to somewhere new;
Till there was n't a star in the dusted fire,
Eastern or western, lower or higher,
But had blinked along each silly spire.

So Yunus, the small man, bald and brown,
Entered this clock-ridden Gnoster-town.
His watch ran well; 't was a gift from the king;
A quaint, old-fashioned sort of thing,

With a rough and wrinkled leathern case,
As if it copied from his face
The parchment wrinkles there, well-earned,
The spectrum-lines where life had burned.
It seemed with salt-brine crusted dim,
But safe within the rusty rim
Its bright, clean wheels ran true and trim,
And steadily by the steady sun
With cheery tick their race went on.
No need had he that another tell
The hour which the deep sky told so well,
For still was the rough-faced watch kept true
By the golden furrow across the blue.

Through the gate and up the street
Trod Yunus with unresting feet.
'T was three o'clock; he was belated;
In Gnoster dinner never waited.
But lo ! he stops in dumb amaze :
The swarm of clocks confronts his gaze.
Some ticked loud, and some ticked soft;
One seemed to wheeze, another coughed;
And their thousand hands gave out that soon
Their thousand throats would bellow noon.

Then Yunus saw, what dazed him more,
That each man motionless stood by his door,
Holding his watch in his open hand,
As a carved tobacconist's man might stand,
Waiting breathlessly to see
If his time with the great town-clocks agree.

Then a silent laugh just pushed its way
Over Yunus' face of wrinkled clay,
Like a gleam of sun on a cloudy day.
And he asked of a citizen standing near,
" Pray, which is the standard time-piece here ? "
" Oh ! well, there 's a many of 'em," quoth he,
" So we strike an average, and agree
Once a week, by majority.
If some seem getting rather slow,
Nor any progressive zeal can show,
We touch 'em up a little, you know ;
And if some are ahead, and seem to lack
Conservative sense, we set 'em back."

Then Yunus stammered : " Should n't you say
That this was rather a dubious way ?
And don't you really happen to know
That your time is at least three hours too slow ? "

The man winked wildly with both his eyes
In a kind of horrified surprise,
Gasped once or twice like a shower-bathed wight,
Then, utterly speechless, took to flight.

And then to a boy : " My little lad,
Are these Gnoster people all stark mad ?
Those clocks are three hours too slow ! " he
said.
But the frightened urchin screamed and ran,
And running he screamed that here was a man
Who doubted and flouted the Gnoster clocks.
And forth the populace rushed in flocks,

With threat and curse and club, pell-mell,
All eager to rout the infidel.

    Well, Yunus thought that his watch was right ;
But, rather than make a scene, or fight,
He hid himself till the wrath died down,
Then hired him a lodging in Gnoster-town.
Yet he never could snatch a quiet walk
But the streets were hissing with muttered talk;
The urchins followed him with stones,
The elders filled the air with groans,
As they watched, those steady streets along,
The wretch who thought their clocks were wrong.

    Then Yunus, taking himself to task,
Began to pluck his beard, and ask,
" O heretic, O hapless wight !
Can a thousand be wrong, and one be right ?
O Yunus, Yunus ! they must be true,
For there 's more of them than there is of you ! "

    Ofttimes he thought he would climb, next day,
To that mountain summit, high away,
Still, unvisited, cold, severe,
Like a soul that is far from earth, and near
To the starry spaces, vast and clear.
" And there, lift up alone," thought he,
" That heaven's true hour mine eyes may see,
A dial I will build for me ;
A marble cube, all carven square,
With a silver gnomon, white and fair,
Down which the good sun, calm and sure,

Shall point the hours with finger pure.
And power to my life that light shall bring
To beat with the wide world's rhythmic swing."
  But more and more it seemed to him
That his own conviction was a whim.
And yet, as it fell out, ere long,
In spite of their being a thousand strong,
His lonely thought was right, they wrong.

  For weeks he slept when his own watch said
'T was the proper time for going to bed,
And he waked at the kiss of the dawn's first beams,
While the Gnoster people were deep in dreams.

  At first it was a pleasant thing
To hear the dawn's first preluding,
Till the tinkle of starlight died away,
And the golden trumpet-blast of day,
Clanging all up the eastern gray,
Broke on a hollow, silent world;
And to see the banneret flowers unfurled
From the battlements of the turf, and own
A new earth, lit for him alone.
His eyes were clear, his soul all free
To stand at Nature's mother-knee,
And greet, with reverent forehead bare,
His brothers of the sky and air.

  But slowly he had lost that tone;
'T was something still and ghostly grown,
And dull, to be up so long alone;
A little chilly, too, withal,

While each long shadow seemed a pall;
And being of too weak a mood
To feed on Nature as a food,
It turned him somewhat faint, at last,
To wait till the village broke its fast.
So the hollow goneness, hunger-lined,
His little courage undermined.
He gave it up, abjured, confessed,
Took him a business, made much pelf,
Laid by his watch on a dusty shelf,
And kept his squints at the sun to himself;
Even gained a place from the orthodox
As winder to one of the public clocks.

   So for many a day it ran;
He had changed his time, but it changed the man.
There were flesh-pots plenty and stoups of wine,
But no more solitudes divine —
No gaze towards the mountain height afar —
No friendship with the beckoning star.

   " All very well," you'll say, and take
The ground, " What difference does it make
What hour we eat, or sleep, or wake ? "
But the Lord of Mhundus thought not so.
He had observed, with inward woe,
That, what with tobacco, wealth, and rum,
And natural heaviness with some,
Great sloth his realm had overcome.
So an edict, which was framed to fix
The rising hour at half-past six,

Throughout the land he caused to go;
And then, the law's success to know,
He took a trip incognito.
   You guess the sequel. Happening round
At Gnoster after nine, he found
The village sunk in sleep profound —
One choral snore the only sound;
Save where, o'erhead, the clocks, sedate,
Stupid and solemn, little and great,
Went ticking on, three hours too late.

   The royal wrath was deep and wide:
He called a magician to his side,
Who swift his hocus-pocus plied,
And laid a thrice-inwoven spell
On the Gnoster sleepers, deep and well.
Not a soul of them waked forevermore,
And some who are versed in ancient lore
Say when it thunders you hear them snore.

   Ah! if only Yunus had held his own,
Though they were a thousand and he alone!
For had he been up, that morning bland,
He, faithful alone to the king's command,
Had risen a duke by the royal hand.
But he let it be as it was to be,
And was doomed with the great majority.

   All the king's sages then searched to see
How in the world it could possibly be,
When the noon was so simple a thing to find,
That a town should stay three hours behind.

It was found they had fetched the time of day
From a place three hundred leagues away —
An hour too slow, of course, nor thought
Of getting their own from the sky as they ought.
Then a timid bird, a poor scared thing,
Flying on panic-stricken wing
Past the clock on the great church tower,
Brushed back its hand another hour;
And at last, by their average method blind,
They had crept the third long hour behind.

To finish the story, let me say
What the court preacher preached next day.

"Don't borrow a creed from other people,
Nor hang most faith on the stoutest steeple.
Look up for your law, but oh! look higher
Than the hands on any human spire.
If ten think alike, and you think alone,
That never proves 't is ten to one
They are right, you wrong; for truth, you see,
Is not a thing of majority.
It never can make you false, them true,
That there 's more of them than there is of you:
If your touch is on Truth's garment's hem,
There is more of you than a world of them.
'T is not alone in the Orient region
That a certain hero's name is Legion.
Nor was it only for once to be
That the whole herd together ran down to the
    sea.

Your zenith for no man else is true;
Your beam from the sun comes alone to you;
And the thought the great God gave your brain,
Is your own for the world, or the world's in vain."

Horae pereunt et imputantur.

THE LOST BIRD

WHAT cared she for the free hearts ? She would com-
fort
The prisoned one :
What recked I of the wanton other singers ?
She sang for me alone —
Was all my own, my own !

But when they loaded me with heavier fetters,
And chained I lay,
How could she know I longed to reach her window ?
Athirst the livelong day,
At eve she fled away.

Still stands her cage wide open at the casement,
In sun and rain,
Though years have gone, and rust has thickly gath-
ered, —
My watching all in vain ;
She will not come again.

Against its wires I strum with idle fingers
From morn to noon ;
I swing the door with loitering touch, and listen
To hear that old-time tune,
Sweet as the soul of June.

My bird, my silver voice that cheered my prison,
   Hushed, lost to me :
And still I wait for death, in chains, forsaken,
   (Soon may the summons be !)
   But she is free.
      — " Is free ? "

Nay, in the palace porches caught and hanging,
   Who says 't is gay,
The song the false prince hears ? who says her sing-
  ing,
   From day to summer day,
   Grieves not her heart away ?

But when my dream comes true in that last sleeping,
   And death makes free,
Against the blue shall snowy wings come sweeping,
   My bird flown back to me,
   Mine for eternity !

SUMMER RAIN

I SAID, " Blue heaven " (Oh, it was beautiful!)
" Send me a tent to shut me to myself:
I am all lonely for my soul, that wanders
Weary, bewildered, beckoned by thy depths;
Thy white, round clouds, great bubbles of creamy
       snow;
Thy luscious sunshine, like some ripe, gold fruit;
Thy songs of birds, and wind warm with the flowers."

And there swept down (Oh, it was beautiful!)
A tent of silver rain, that fell like a veil
Shutting me in to think all quiet thoughts,
And feel the vibrant thrill of shadowy wings
That fluttered, checking their swift flight, and hear,
Though with no syllable of earthly music,
A voice of melody unutterable.

THE BELLOWS–BOY

I BLOW the organ at St. Timothy's.
Did you know 't was not the master, after all,
(I used to think so, too) that speaks the great
Sweet sounds ? He only beckons at the keys,
And God's winds come and sing for him; while I,
I draw the great winds in from up the air.
'T is hard, I tell you! Sometimes they hold back,
And make me tug and strain to draw them in.
But then they always come : all except once,
When I forgot to do my work.

                              You see,
'T was a wild night, and after church was done,
The dear old voices had been battling hard,
Near drowned in storm and sea, and had got forth
Out of the roar and whirl, and on the beach
Lay panting, while the waves died into sobs,
Leaving them lying, watching the soft foam. —
I fell to dreaming with them, listening
How the blue water plashed, quiet and far,
Till, of a sudden, a horrible, drawn wail,
Then silence, out of which I started, dazed,
At a fierce red face and raging whisper, " Blow ! "

They took my work away, for that; but soon
I begged and begged it back again, and now
I try to tug so hard as not to hear.

Sometimes I creep round nights, when the choir is
        gone,
And stealthily unlock the carved oak doors,
To flatten my hand along the ivory keys,
As smooth and chill as ice. They will not speak, —
The smooth white lips, yet always I hear tunes,
Back in the empty dark, and over me
In the gold pipes: it may be my own thoughts,
Playing at music. One I always hear
That hangs in the dark like a great white flower, and
        there
It grows and fades.

                        For, once, the minister
(Him with the great high forehead), Christmas Day,
Walked down the alley, and stopped, and spoke to
        me
(Faith! but I shook, though, when his steady hand
Stayed on my head a minute), and he said
That even the master, and he, and every one —
Even the beautiful people in the choir —
Only did work like mine, moved hands or lips,
While the music all was God's, and came from
        Him.

So, ever since, it has come into my tunes,
That maybe in *that* world I can make sounds
Like the great, sweet ones, and may have white keys
All of my own, and not so cold and dumb,
Nights, when I touch them!

THE NEW YEAR

Go, minister of God,
To drowsy pews where nod
Your flock, who know so well
The empty tale you tell !
Some morning go and dare
Speak what your real thoughts are, —
See them awake, and stare !
Go, father, to your sons, —
Yea, to those milder ones,
The daughters, soft and meek ;
And after sermon speak
No half-truths, told with tact,
But what you think is fact.
Go, wielder of the pen !
Write for your fellow-men
What you have hinted true
In whispers to a few.

But you must look to see
What present loss 't will be ?
Ah, wielder of the pen,
They will not praise you then !
Ah, minister of — Whom ? —
There will be sudden room

In every velvet pew,
If you but once speak true.
Shame on you, cowards all!
Is God's great throne to fall
Except you prop it round
With your poor empty sound?
Think ye you'll ne'er be fed
Unless, by Satan led,
You bid your stones be bread?
You think the universe
Goes on from bad to worse,
And with some glittering bait
You'll coax it from its fate?
You think all truth was given
To you from cautious heaven,
To keep beneath your thumb,
And dole out, crumb by crumb,
Lest haply, if once known,
The world were overthrown?
The world — O faithless clod!
Who made it, — you, or God?
Ah, well, this seems His way:
He made the cowards, too;
He leaves the false with true —
He leaves it till the day
When suddenly men shall say,
"What! you were one, — and you?
It was no scattered few?
Why not, if we all knew,

Have told each other so,
Openly, long ago ? "

Yes : let us understand,
Now, on whose side we stand, —
The poor old man's at Rome,
Good but to feebly foam
At each new torch men light,
Encroaching on his night;
Or theirs, who find God's way
By no dark lantern's ray,
But in the light of day.

Of all the pillars fair
Holding the world in air,
Canst thou one shaft espy
Based on a crafty lie ?
Is but one column there
A sham, an empty shell ?
Not one ? Then hew away,
All good right arms that may:
No falsehood we can fell
Holds up God's citadel.
For every cheat that falls,
The firmer stand the walls.
For all that 's cleared away
Of rubbish and decay,
The sounder stand and shine
The square-hewn walls divine.

O younger souls! for you
'T is easy to be true.
Dear spirit, far or near
Let this new-risen year
Be a new birth to thee;
Stand forth — be wholly free.
Count not what it shall cost, —
Given for the world — not lost,
Deep down within thy heart,
If thou dost feel it start, —
Some longing to be free,
Some fresh fidelity,
Some blush upon the cheek
For all the past, so weak;
Some manlier will to dare, —
If thou dost feel it stir,
Grieve not the messenger:
Thy better angel there
Thou hearest, unaware.

THE TRUANT

"Sent out, was I, to turn the sod?
  What waste of such a day!
Who would not, under blue like that,
  Fling the old spade away?
If they but knew the ripples' plash,
  And loved the lark as I!
How could one dig, and half the time
  Gaze at the luscious sky?
Better to watch my dipping kite
  Go swaying up the cloud,
Or mock the tireless thrush, or shout
  My own free songs aloud."

So half the day he gazed, and wished
  The tugging kite to be,
And wondered if that endless sky
  Was not eternity.
Or, tossing snowy pebbles out
  Beyond the lake's gray rim,
He stood to watch the ripple-ranks
  Come ringing back to him.

Was it, I wonder, loitering there
  Only an idle boy?

Or was it a poet, claiming so
   His heritage of joy?
Who watched above the rounded world
   His fancy float and swim,
Or tossed his dreams out, watching men's
   Brave deeds ring back to him.

SPRING

WHEN is it Spring? When spirits rise,
Pure crocus-buds, where the snow dies;
When children play outdoors till dark;
When the sap trickles up the bark;
When bits of blue sky flit and sing,
Playing at birds — then is it Spring?

When is it Spring? When the bee hums;
When through the opened window comes
The breeze, and summer-license claims
To swing and toss the picture frames;
When the walk dries; the robins call;
The brown hens doze by the sunny wall,
One foot drawn up to warm, or sing,
With half-filmed eyes — then is it Spring?

Nay, each might prove a treacherous sign:
But when old waters seem new wine;
When all our mates are half divine;
When love comes easier than hate;
When we have no more shrugs at Fate,
But think sometimes of God, and late
Our swiftest serving seems to be;
When bright ways numberless we see,

And thoughts spring up, and hopes run free,
And wild new dreams are all on wing,
Till we must either fly or sing
With riotous life — be sure 't is Spring.

TRANQUILLITY

WEARY, and marred with care and pain
And bruising days, the human brain
Draws wounded inward, — it might be
Some delicate creature of the sea,
That, shuddering, shrinks its lucent dome,
And coils its azure tendrils home,
And folds its filmy curtains tight
At jarring contact, e'er so light;
But let it float away all free,
And feel the buoyant, supple sea
Among its tinted streamers swell,
Again it spreads its gauzy wings,
And, waving its wan fringes, swings
With rhythmic pulse its crystal bell.

So let the mind, with care o'erwrought,
Float down the tranquil tides of thought:
Calm visions of unending years
Beyond this little moment's fears;
Of boundless regions far from where
The girdle of the azure air
Binds to the earth the prisoned mind.
Set free the fancy, till it find
Beyond our world a vaster place

To thrill and vibrate out through space, —
As some auroral banner streams
Up through the night in pulsing gleams,
And floats and flashes o'er our dreams;
There let the whirling planet fall
Down — down, till but a glimmering ball,
A misty star: and dwindled so,
There is no room for care, or woe,
Or wish, apart from that one Will
That doth the worlds with music fill.

IN A FAR COUNTRY

Once, in a dream, in a bleak, sea-blown land,
  A man wreck-stranded many a month before
  Saw for a moment — not the broken oar,
Nor sand-sunk keel; nor wild men that would stand
With uncouth gibberish on either hand
  If he walked forth, or peered about the door
  Where stretched he lay on his rude hut's beach-
     floor;
Nor heard the dull waves fretting at the sand:

But heard once more, this blessed dream within,
  The mother-tongue heard not these many years,
    And old familiar motions had their power;
Saw, for once more, the faces of his kin,
  And took their hands, half-laughing, half in tears,
    And it was home, home, home, for this one
     hour.

THE WONDERFUL THOUGHT

It comes upon me in the woods,
  Of all the days, this day in May :
When wind and rain can never think
  Whose turn 't is now to have its way.

It finds me as I lie along,
  Blinking up through the swaying trees,
Half wondering if a man who reads
  " Blue sky " in books *that* color sees, —

So fathomless and pure : as if
  All loveliest azure things have gone
To heaven that way, — the flowers, the sea, —
  And left their color there alone.

Hark ! leaning on each other's arms,
  The pines are whispering in the breeze,
Whispering, — then hushing, half in awe
  Their legends of primeval seas.

The wild things of the wood come out,
  And stir or hide, as wild things will,
Like thoughts that may not be pursued,
  But come if one is calm and still.

Deep hemlocks down the gorge shut in
　Their caves with hollow shadow filled,
Where little feathered anchorites
　Behind a sunlit lattice build.

And glimmering through that lace of boughs,
　Dancing, while they hang darker still,
Along the restful river shines
　The restless light's incessant thrill:

As in some sober, silent soul,
　Whose life appears a tranquil stream,
Through some unguarded rift you catch
　The wildest wishes, all agleam.

But to my thought — so wonderful!
　I know if once 't were told, all men
Would feel it warm at heart, and life
　Be more than it had ever been.

'T would make these flowerless woods laugh out
　With every garden-color bright,
Where only, now, the dogwood hangs
　Its scattered cloud of ghostly white.

Those birds would hold no more aloof: —
　How know they I am here, so well?
'T is yon woodpecker's warning note;
　He is their seer and sentinel.

They use him, but his faithfulness
  Perchance in human fashion pay, —
Laugh in their feathers at his voice,
  And ridicule his stumbling way.

That far-off flute-note — hours in vain
  I 've followed it, so shy and fleet;
But if I found him, well I know
  His song would seem not half so sweet.

The swift, soft creatures, — how I wish
  They 'd trust me, and come perch upon
My shoulders ! Do they guess that then
  Their charm would be forever gone ?

But still I prate of sight and sound;
  Ah, well, 't is always so in rhyme ;
The idle fancies find a voice,
  The wise thought waits — another time.

TO "THE RADICAL"

1871

AFTER sleep, the waking;
After night, dawn breaking;
After silence long,
A burst of song.
We knew thou wert not gone,
To leave us without champion —
Our first free voice 'mid servile tongues
And secret sneers and bigot wrongs:
With good Thor-hammer beating down
The tyrant lie with tinsel crown;
With message, now unsealed again,
Of love to God in love to men.
Who calls thy manner cold as snow?
Can pure spring have the summer's glow,
Or crocus-buds like roses blow?
Who says the dawn is vague and gray?
So clear, the sight can reach away
To stainless peaks that shine afar
And dim beyond the morning star.
Choose who may the summer noon,
Longing to be let alone, —
Force unstrung, and vigor gone.

Welcome the sweet breath of Spring!
Morning air to tempt the wing;
Distance, cool and clear and still,
For the eye to pierce at will.
Welcome, O vanward voice!
Sound on! Be strong! Rejoice!
And so, in thy fresh history,
Foretell the world-old mystery,
Hinting what is to be
For us, as now for thee.
After sleep, the waking;
After night, dawn breaking;
After silence long,
A burst of song.

THE INVISIBLE

If there is naught but what we see,
What is the wide world worth to me?
But is there naught save what we see?
A thousand things on every hand
My sense is numb to understand:
I know we eddy round the sun;
When has it dizzied any one?
I know the round worlds draw from far,
Through hollow systems, star to star;
But who has e'er upon a strand
Of those great cables laid his hand?
What reaches up from room to room
Of chambered earth, through glare or gloom,
Through molten flood and fiery blast,
And binds our hurrying feet so fast?
'T is the earth-mother's love, that well
Will hold the motes that round her dwell:
Through granite hills you feel it stir
As lightly as through gossamer:
Its grasp unseen by mortal eyes,
Its grain no lens can analyze.

If there is naught but what we see,
The friend I loved is lost to me :
He fell asleep ; who dares to say
His spirit is so far away ?
Who knows what wings are round about ?
These thoughts — who proves but from without
They still are whispered ? Who can think
They rise from morning's food and drink !
These thoughts that stream on like the sea,
And darkly beat incessantly
The feet of some great hope, and break,
And only broken glimmers make,
Nor ever climb the shore, to lie
And calmly mirror the far sky,
And image forth in tranquil deeps
The secret that its silence keeps.

Because he never comes, and stands
And stretches out to me both hands,
Because he never leans before
The gate, when I set wide the door
At morning, nor is ever found
Just at my side when I turn round,
Half thinking I shall meet his eyes,
From watching the broad moon-globe rise, —
For all this, shall I homage pay
To Death, grow cold of heart, and say,
" He perished, and has ceased to be ;

Another comes, but never he " ?
Nay, by our wondrous being, nay !
Although his face I never see
Through all the infinite To Be,
I know he lives and cares for me.

A DRIFTING CLOUD

Born of the shadows that it passes through,
    Incessantly becoming and destroyed,
Its form unchanged, its substance ever new,
    Builded from its own largess to the void;
Of steady purpose innerly aware,
Yet blindly borne upon the streaming air, —

Giving itself away, distributing
    Its own abundant heart in splendid showers,
But not impoverished, since its losses bring
    Perpetual renewing all the hours:
Drifting, sunlit or shadowed, to the sea, —
O cloud, thou hast a human destiny !

A REPLY

To the mother of the world,
Not for help or light or grace,
Basely I for comfort came:
And I brought my craven fears,
Late amends of useless tears,
Brought my stumbling feet so lame,
Hopes with weary pinions furled,
Every longing unattained,
All my love with self-love stained, —
Told them to her grave, mild face.

And the mother of the world
Spake, and answered unto me,
In the brook that past me purled;
In the bluebird's heavenly hue,
When beyond his downward swerve
Up he glanced, a sweep of blue;
In the sunshine's shifting spray,
Drifted in beneath the tree
Where I sheltered, lest its flood
There outside should drown my blood;
In the cloud-pearl's melting curve;
In the little odorous thrill
Trembling from each blossom-bell;

In the silence of the sky,
And the thoughts that from it fell,
Floating as a snowflake will, —
So the mother answered me:

" Child ! it is not thine to see
Why at all thy life should be,
Wherefore thou must thus abide,
Foiled, repulsed, unsatisfied.
Thou hast not to prove thy right
To the earth-room and the light.
Thou hast not to justify
Thought of mine to human eye.
I have borne thee ! Trust to me !
Strength and help are in thy deed;
Comfort thou shalt scorn to need.
Careless what shall come to thee,
Look but what thy work shall be."

THE SCHOOLHOUSE WINDOWS

HOPE builded herself a palace
 At the heart of the oak-roofed town,
And out of its airy windows
 Her happy eyes looked down:

Her eyes — the beautiful eyes of Hope —
 All day were shining there,
And the morning heard her merry songs
 Ring out on the fresh sea-air.

Full many a changing face has she
 For the changing earth below,
And to each the magical windows
 A different picture show.

As when you stand in the twilight
 And watch through the darkling pane,
Till the image of your face appears
 Against the fading plain,

And a wider world is opened, —
 The ghost of the firelit room
That wavers and glows and glimmers
 Beyond in the hollow gloom, —

Till, out through the mirrored phantoms,
  The stars and the spectral trees
Are the dim and columned corridors
  Of wonderful palaces,

So each of the childish faces
  That looks out into the air,
Through an image of itself must see
  That colors all things there;

And the hill and the azure water
  Can never be twice the same,
For the hue of the seeing eye will tint
  Its vision in dust or flame.

Our lives are but what we see them;
  Bright, if the eye-beams are : —
Not what shines in, but what shines out,
  Makes every world a star.

So when at the schoolhouse windows
  They stand, the guileless wise,
I peer o'er the clustered shoulders,
  And see with their own bright eyes.

Then the vanishing mists of morning
  Like airy portals ope,
And the hills that lift their slopes beyond
  Are the boundless realms of Hope.

The slim ships, out of the western haze,
   Come moving, dim and still,
As if the sights of the solemn sea
   Had awed them like a spell.

And as a quiet, land-locked bay
   Their schooldays seem to be,
And they long, through the gate of golden years,
   To pass to the world's wide sea.

Then we look from the sunny windows
   On the lives that plod below,
Who guess not how, to us, their ways
   'Twixt blooming gardens go ;

And we see how every toiling life
   May look serene and fair,
If the soul but climb above itself
   And gaze from the upper air.

But the master, after school is done,
   And the children are all away,
He reads in the window-panes the thoughts
   That have winged from them all day.

As he watches the loud troop homeward,
   Till the pattering feet are still,
He reads the innocent musings
   That the crystal tablets fill.

There one had leaned and listened,
  And heard in the empty air
Invisible armies marching
  To the soundless trumpet's blare.

And one had caught the motion
  Of the great world round the sun,
Till he felt on his face the rush of space
  As the whirling Earth-ball spun.

The dream and the aspiration;
  The glimpse of the higher home;
The noble scorn of the world that is,
  And the worship of that to come:

The thirst for a life diviner,
  And the sigh of self-despair,
That rose through the blue to the gate of heaven
  And was answered like a prayer.

Ah, for him the panes are crowded
  With the volumes of such lore,
And the children will catch, to-morrow,
  The glimmers of days before;

Till the dry and dreary lesson
  In luminous letters shines,
Where the magical schoolhouse windows
  Have written between the lines.

But the brightest of all the windows
   In the palace of Hope so fair,
Are the eyes where merry thoughts climb up
   And beckon each other there.

There are clear and sea-blue windows
   Behind whose pencilled bars
The bright hours are all sunshine,
   And the dark ones lit with stars:

And there are shady casements,
   That gentle secrets keep,
And you seek in vain through the clouded pane
   If the spirit wake or sleep:

And oriels gray, where, cool and still,
   The soul leans out to see,
As you shape for the prince the sword and crown
   Of the king that is to be.

The years of the unknown future
   Even now are on the wing,
Like a flight of beautiful singing birds
   From the distance hastening.

O children, O blind musicians,
   With powers beyond your ken,
Moulding, but guessing not, the souls
   That shall wear your faces then —

Shall the look be clear with truth, or drear
   And hollow with mocking days?
Shall the eyes be sweet with the love of man,
   Or shrunk with the lust of praise?

And what, from those future windows,
   Shall the magical pictures be? —
The scattered wrecks of fleets of care,
   Or a blessed argosy?

Perchance when ye come and stand and muse
   On the years that were half in vain,
A mist that is not of the ocean born
   May be blurring the window-pane.

And one may sigh to remember
   The old-time wishes there,
And the bows of empty promise
   That have broken in the air.

And some shall wonder and wonder,
   As they think of the days of old,
How their world from the schoolhouse windows
   Could have looked so bare and cold:

For the mist that was thick at morning,
   From the noon shall have risen and fled,
And the air shall be full of fragrance now,
   From the blossoms that it fed.

O friends, have the paths grown empty?
  Do the winds play out of tune?
Have the early gleams of glory gone
  From the sober afternoon?

Then follow the little footprints
  Out from your care and pain,
And the world from the schoolhouse windows
  Will look all young again.

Oh, the never-forgotten schooldays!
  Whose music, fresh and pure,
Is woven of hints of songs to come,
  Like a beautiful overture —

When the spirit had not touched its bounds
  Of weakness or of sin,
But the nebulous light was round it still
  Of the soul it might have been.

Oh, the old earth will be Eden,
  Fairer than that of yore,
When the young hearts all shall grow to be
  What the good God meant them for!

We are all but His schoolchildren,
  And earth is our schoolhouse now,
Where duties are set for lessons —
  Whose windows are midnight's blue.

And out through that starry casement,
  Some night when the skies are clear,
We shall watch the mists of time lift up
  And the hills of heaven appear.

A FOOLISH WISH

Why need I seek some burden small to bear
       Before I go?
Will not a host of nobler souls be here,
       Heaven's will to do?
Of stronger hands, unfailing, unafraid?
O silly soul! what matters my small aid
       Before I go!

I tried to find, that I might show to them,
       Before I go,
The path of purer lives: the light was dim,
       I do not know
If I had found some footprints of the way;
It is too late their wandering feet to stay,
       Before I go.

I would have sung the rest some song of cheer,
       Before I go.
But still the chords rang false; some jar of fear,
       Some jangling woe.
And at the end I cannot weave one chord
To float into their hearts my last warm word,
       Before I go.

I would be satisfied if I might tell,
     Before I go,
That one warm word, — how I have loved them well,
     Could they but know!
And would have gained for them some gleam of
     good;
Have sought it long; still seek, — if but I could!
     Before I go.

'T is a child's longing, on the beach at play:
     " Before I go,"
He begs the beckoning mother, " Let me stay
     One shell to throw!"
'T is coming night; the great sea climbs the shore, —
" Ah, let me toss one little pebble more,
     Before I go!"

THE SECRET

A TIDE of sun and song in beauty broke
Against a bitter heart, where no voice woke
  Till thus it spoke : —

What was it, in the old time that I know,
That made the world with inner beauty glow,
  Now a vain show ?

Still dance the shadows on the grass at play,
Still move the clouds like great, calm thoughts away,
  Nor haste, nor stay.

But I have lost that breath within the gale,
That light to which the daylight was a veil,
  The star-shine pale.

Still all the summer with its songs is filled,
But that delicious undertone they held —
  Why is it stilled ?

Then I took heart that I would find again
The voices that had long in silence lain,
  Nor live in vain.

I stood at noonday in the hollow wind,
Listened at midnight, straining heart and mind
    If I might find!

But all in vain I sought, at eve and morn,
On sunny seas, in dripping woods forlorn,
    Till tired and worn,

One day I left my solitary tent
And down into the world's bright garden went,
    On labor bent.

The dew stars and the buds about my feet
Began their old bright message to repeat,
    In odors sweet;

And as I worked at weed and root in glee,
Now humming and now whistling cheerily,
    It came to me, —

The secret of the glory that was fled
Shone like a sweep of sun all overhead,
    And something said, —

" The blessing came because it was not sought;
There was no care if thou were blest or not:
The beauty and the wonder all thy thought, —
    Thyself forgot."

POEMS WRITTEN BETWEEN
1872 AND 1880

THE THINGS THAT WILL NOT DIE

WHAT am I glad will stay when I have passed
  From this dear valley of the world, and stand
On yon snow-glimmering peaks, and lingering cast
      From that dim land
  A backward look, and haply stretch my hand,
Regretful, now the wish comes true at last?

Sweet strains of music I am glad will be
  Still wandering down the wind, for men will hear
And think themselves from all their care set free,
      And heaven near
  When summer stars burn very still and clear,
And waves of sound are swelling like the sea.

And it is good to know that overhead
  Blue skies will brighten, and the sun will shine,
And flowers be sweet in many a garden bed,
      And all divine
  (For are they not, O Father, thoughts of thine?)
Earth's warmth and fragrance shall on men be shed.

And I am glad that Night will always come,
  Hushing all sounds, even the soft-voiced birds,
Putting away all light from her deep dome,
          Until are heard
  In the wide starlight's stillness, unknown words,
That make the heart ache till it find its home.

And I am glad that neither golden sky,
  Nor violet lights that linger on the hill,
Nor ocean's wistful blue shall satisfy,
          But they shall fill
  With wild unrest and endless longing still
The soul whose hope beyond them all must lie.

And I rejoice that love shall never seem
  So perfect as it ever was to be,
But endlessly that inner haunting dream
          Each heart shall see
  Hinted in every dawn's fresh purity,
Hopelessly shadowed in each sunset's gleam.

And though warm mouths will kiss and hands will
          cling,
  And thought by silent thought be understood,
I do rejoice that the next hour will bring
          That far-off mood,
  That drives one like a lonely child to God,
Who only sees and measures everything.

And it is well that when these feet have pressed
   The outward path from earth, 't will not seem sad
To them to stay ; but they who love me best
          Will be most glad
   That such a long unquiet now has had,
At last, a gift of perfect peace and rest.

A CHILD AND A STAR

THE star, so pure in saintly white,
Deep in the solemn soul of night,
With dreams of deathless beauty wed,
And golden ways that seraphs tread :
The child — so mere a thing of earth,
So meek a flower of mortal birth :
A far-off lucent world, so bright,
Stooping to touch with tender light
That little gown at evening prayer :
It seems a condescension rare, —
Heaven round a common child to glow !
Ah ! wiser eyes of angels know
The star, a toy but roughly wrought ;
The child, God's own most loving thought.
Yon evening planet, wan with moons,
Colossal, 'mid its dim, swift noons, —
What is it but a bulk of stone,
Like this gray globe we dwell upon ?
Down hollow spaces, sightless, chill,
Its vibrant beams in darkness thrill,
Till through some window drift the rays
Where a pure heart looks up and prays ;
And in that silent worshiper,
The waves of feeling stir and stir,

And spread in wider rings above,
To tremble at God's heart of love.
Though it be kingliest one of all
His worlds, 't is but a stony ball:
What are they all, from sun to sun,
But dust and stubble, when all 's done?
Some heavenly grace it only caught,
When, like a hint from home, it brought
To a child's heart one tender thought:
Itself in that great mystery lost,
As some bright pebble, idly tost
Into the darkling sea at night,
Whose widening ripples, running light,
Go out into the infinite.

REVERIE

Whether 't was in that dome of evening sky,
  So hollow where the few great stars were bright,
Or something in the cricket's lonely cry,
  Or, farther off, where swelled upon the night
  The surf-beat of the symphony's delight,
Then died in crumbling cadences away —
A dream of Schubert's soul, too sweet to stay:

Whether from these, or secret spell within, —
  It seemed an empty waste of endless sea,
Where the waves mourned for what had never been,
  Where the wind sought for what could never be:
  Then all was still, in vast expectancy
Of powers that waited but some mystic sign
To touch the dead world to a life divine.

Me, too, it filled — that breathless, blind desire;
  And every motion of the oars of thought
Thrilled all the deep in flashes — sparks of fire
  In meshes of the darkling ripples caught.
  Swiftly rekindled, and then quenched to naught;
And the dark held me; wish and will were none:
A soul unformed and void, silent, alone,
And brooded over by the Infinite One.

IS IT SAFE?

Two souls, whose bodies sate them on a hill,
And, beating idly on a stone, one said:

"Yes, light is good, and air; but were it well
To burst the walls that keep the Terror out?
Let faith, my one great pearl, bide deep in the dark,
If love, its lustre, will be dulled in the sun.
See, now: a darkness round us in the world,—
This tossing world that rides upon the waves;
A glimmer overhead; the wrath and roar
Of awful waters rushing thunderously.
Slaves, penned in the pitch-dark hold, shall we go
      wild
To crush the planks through, mad for light and
      air,
And drawn in the swirling gulf of that despair?
Better to wait, and guess the end is good,
And hope in some great angel at the helm,
Poring on the mystic words they dropped —
Those dreaming shipmates, that these many nights
Have muttered in their dreams and prophesied."

The other — grim, with eyes of fathomless trust —
Thus spake:

" A darkness round the sparrow's egg;
A warm thin wall; within a downy throb —
A fluttering heart. Strange noises swell, or swoon,
Outside that amber glimmer arching round.
The wind rocks bough and nest and mother bird;
The timid heart waits in a dizzy awe;
All things seem rushing like a roaring sea.
It struggles; shall it dare break through the wall —
This safe, smooth wall, so wisely built for it —
And let the unknown Terror in, and die ?
With chip on chip of tiny crusted bill
The wall is cleft, and — lo ! on perfumed wings
The sun leaps in with a laugh; the dancing leaves
Hang merrily beckoning, and blossom-boughs
Nod gayly to the whispering summer air."

FIVE LIVES

FIVE mites of monads dwelt in a round drop
That twinkled on a leaf by a pool in the sun.
To the naked eye they lived invisible;
Specks, for a world of whom the empty shell
Of a mustard-seed had been a hollow sky.

One was a meditative monad, called a sage;
And, shrinking all his mind within, he thought:
"Tradition, handed down for hours and hours,
Tells that our globe, this quivering crystal world,
Is slowly dying. What if, seconds hence,
When I am very old, yon shimmering dome
Come drawing down and down, till all things end?"
Then with a weazen smirk he proudly felt
No other mote of God had ever gained
Such giant grasp of universal truth.

One was a transcendental monad; thin
And long and slim in the mind; and thus he mused:
"Oh, vast, unfathomable monad-souls!
Made in the image" — a hoarse frog croaks from the
        pool —
"Hark! 't was some god, voicing his glorious thought
In thunder music! Yea, we hear their voice,

And we may guess their minds from ours, their work.
Some taste they have like ours, some tendency
To wriggle about, and munch a trace of scum."
He floated up on a pin-point bubble of gas
That burst, pricked by the air, and he was gone.

One was a barren-minded monad, called
A positivist; and he knew positively :
" There is no world beyond this certain drop.
Prove me another! Let the dreamers dream
Of their faint dreams, and noises from without,
And higher and lower; life is life enough."
Then swaggering half a hair's breadth, hungrily
He seized upon an atom of bug, and fed.

One was a tattered monad, called a poet ;
And with shrill voice ecstatic thus he sang :
" Oh, the little female monad's lips !
Oh, the little female monad's eyes :
Ah, the little, little, female, female monad ! "

The last was a strong-minded monadess,
Who dashed amid the infusoria,
Danced high and low, and wildly spun and dove
Till the dizzy others held their breath to see.

But while they led their wondrous little lives
Æonian moments had gone wheeling by.
The burning drop had shrunk with fearful speed;

A glistening film — 't was gone; the leaf was dry.
The little ghost of an inaudible squeak
Was lost to the frog that goggled from his stone;
Who, at the huge, slow tread of a thoughtful ox
Coming to drink, stirred sideways fatly, plunged,
Launched backward twice, and all the pool was still.

THE OPEN WINDOW

My tower was grimly builded,
  With many a bolt and bar,
"And here," I thought, "I will keep my life
  From the bitter world afar."

Dark and chill was the stony floor,
  Where never a sunbeam lay,
And the mould crept up on the dreary wall,
  With its ghost touch, day by day.

One morn, in my sullen musings,
  A flutter and cry I heard;
And close at the rusty casement
  There clung a frightened bird.

Then back I flung the shutter
  That was never before undone,
And I kept till its wings were rested
  The little weary one.

But in through the open window,
  Which I had forgot to close,
There had burst a gush of sunshine
  And a summer scent of rose.

For all the while I had burrowed
  There in my dingy tower,
Lo! the birds had sung and the leaves had danced
  From hour to sunny hour.

And such balm and warmth and beauty
  Came drifting in since then,
That window still stands open
  And shall never be shut again.

GOOD NEWS

T IS just the day to hear good news :
   The pulses of the world are still ;
The eager spring's unfolding hues
   Are drowned in floods of sun, that fill
The golden air, and softly bear
Deep sleep and silence everywhere.
   No ripple runs along that sea
Of warm, new grass, but all things wear
   A hush of calm expectancy :
   What is coming to Heart and me ?

The idle clouds, that work their wills
In moods of shadow, on the hills ;
The dusky hollows in the trees,
Veiled with their sunlit 'broideries ;
The gate that has not swung, all day ;
   The dappled water's drowsy gleam ;
The tap of hammers far away,
   And distant voices, like a dream, —
All seem but visions, and a tone
   Haunts them of tidings they refuse :
So, all the quiet afternoon,
Heart and I we sit alone,
   Waiting for some good news.

Other days had life to spare,
　　Tasks to do, and men to meet,
Trifling wishes, bits of care,
　　A hundred ways for ready feet;
　　But this bright day is all so sweet,
So sweet, 't is sad in its content;
As if kind Nature, as she went
Her happy way, had paused a space,
Remembered us, and turned her face
　　As toward some protest of distress;
Waiting till we should find our place
　　In the wide world's happiness.
Nothing stirs but some vague scent,
　　A breath of hidden violet —
The lonely last of odors gone —
　　Still lingering from the morning dews,
As if it were the earth's regret
For other such bright days that went,
While Heart and I we sat alone,
　　Waiting for our good news.

What would you have for your good news,
　　Foolish Heart, O foolish Heart?
Some new freedom to abuse,
　　Some old trouble to depart?
Sudden flash of snowy wing
Out of yonder blue, to bring
Messages so long denied?

The old greeting at your side,
The old hunger satisfied ?

Nay, the distant will not come;
To deaf ears all songs are dumb :
   Silly Heart, O silly Heart !
From within joy must begin —
   What could help the thing thou art ?
Nothing draweth from afar,
The gods can give but what we are.
Heaven makes the mould, but soon and late
Man pours the metal — that is Fate.
We must speak the word we wait,
   And give the gift we die to own.
   Wake, O Heart ! From us alone
      Can come our best good news.

SUNDAY

Not a dread cavern, hoar with damp and mould,
Where I must creep, and in the dark and cold,
   Offer some awful incense at a shrine
   That hath no more divine
Than that 't is far from life, and stern, and old;

But a bright hilltop in the breezy air,
Full of the morning freshness high and clear,
   Where I may climb and drink the pure, new day,
   And see where winds away
The path that God would send me, shining fair.

A BRIGHT HILLTOP IN THE BREEZY AIR

PEACE

'T is not in seeking,
'T is not in endless striving,
   Thy quest is found:
Be still and listen;
Be still and drink the quiet
  Of all around.

Not for thy crying,
Not for thy loud beseeching,
  Will peace draw near:
Rest with palms folded;
Rest with thine eyelids fallen —
  Lo! peace is here.

DARE YOU?

DOUBTING Thomas and loving John,
Behind the others walking on : —

" Tell me now, John, dare you be
One of the minority ?
To be lonely in your thought,
Never visited nor sought,
Shunned with secret shrug, to go
Through the world esteemed its foe ;
To be singled out and hissed,
Pointed at as one unblessed,
Warned against in whispers faint,
Lest the children catch a taint ;
To bear off your titles well, —
Heretic and infidel ?
If you dare, come now with me,
Fearless, confident, and free."

" Thomas, do you dare to be
Of the great majority ?
To be only, as the rest,
With Heaven's common comforts blessed ;
To accept, in humble part,
Truth that shines on every heart ;

Never to be set on high,
Where the envious curses fly ;
Never name or fame to find,
Still outstripped in soul and mind ;
To be hid, unless to God,
As one grass-blade in the sod,
Underfoot with millions trod ?
If you dare, come with us, be
Lost in love's great unity."

CHRISTMAS IN CALIFORNIA

Can this be Christmas — sweet as May,
   With drowsy sun, and dreamy air,
And new grass pointing out the way
   For flowers to follow, everywhere ?

Has time grown sleepy at his post,
   And let the exiled Summer back,
Or is it her regretful ghost,
   Or witchcraft of the almanac ?

While wandering breaths of mignonette
   In at the open window come,
I send my thoughts afar, and let
   Them paint your Christmas Day at home.

Glitter of ice, and glint of frost,
   And sparkles in the crusted snow ;
And hark ! the dancing sleigh-bells, tost
   The faster as they fainter grow.

The creaking footsteps hurry past ;
   The quick breath dims the frosty air ;
And down the crisp road slipping fast
   Their laughing loads the cutters bear.

Penciled against the cold white sky,
   Above the curling eaves of snow,
The thin blue smoke lifts lingeringly,
   As loath to leave the mirth below.

For at the door a merry din
   Is heard, with stamp of feathery feet,
And chattering girls come storming in,
   To toast them at the roaring grate.

And then from muff and pocket peer,
   And many a warm and scented nook,
Mysterious little bundles queer,
   That, rustling, tempt the curious look.

Now broad upon the southern walls
   The mellowed sun's great smile appears,
And tips the rough-ringed icicles
   With sparks, that grow to glittering tears.

Then, as the darkening day goes by,
   The wind gets gustier without,
And leaden streaks are on the sky,
   And whirls of snow are all about.

Soon firelight shadows, merry crew,
   Along the darkling walls will leap
And clap their hands, as if they knew
   A thousand things too good to keep.

Sweet eyes with home's contentment filled,
 As in the smouldering coals they peer,
Haply some wondering pictures build
 Of how I keep my Christmas here.

Before me, on the wide, warm bay,
 A million azure ripples run;
Round me the sprouting palm-shoots lay
 Their shining lances to the sun.

With glossy leaves that poise or swing,
 The callas their white cups unfold,
And faintest chimes of odor ring
 From silver bells with tongues of gold.

A languor of deliciousness
 Fills all the sea-enchanted clime;
And in the blue heavens meet, and kiss,
 The loitering clouds of summer-time.

This fragrance of the mountain balm
 From spicy Lebanon might be;
Beneath such sunshine's amber calm
 Slumbered the waves of Galilee.

O wondrous gift, in goodness given,
 Each hour anew our eyes to greet,
An earth so fair — so close to Heaven,
 'T was trodden by the Master's feet.

And we — what bring we in return?
  Only these broken lives, and lift
Them up to meet His pitying scorn,
  As some poor child its foolish gift:

As some poor child on Christmas Day
  Its broken toy in love might bring;
You could not break its heart and say
  You cared not for the worthless thing?

Ah, word of trust, His child! That child
  Who brought to earth the life divine,
Tells me the Father's pity mild
  Scorns not even such a gift as mine.

I am His creature, and His air
  I breathe, where'er my feet may stand;
The angels' song rings everywhere,
  And all the earth is Holy Land.

BUT FOR HIM

DUMB and still was the heart of man
By the river of Time:
Far it stretched, and wide and free,
This rapid river; on it ran,
Through many a land and many a clime,
On and on, and no tide turned,
Down and down to Eternity.

Dumb and still — but the man's heart yearned
For a voice to break the silence long;
And there by the side of the heart of man
Stood the spirit of Song.

Then the waves laughed
Down the river of Time;
And the west wind and the south wind sang,
And the world was glad,
For now it had
A voice to utter, in jocund chime,
The joy it quaffed
From the river of Time.

But when the song grew low and sad,
The trees drooped,

The flowers were dim,
And a dark cloud down from heaven stooped;
The wind mourned, and tear-drops fell;
And the world cried, grieving, " But for him
We had not known but all was well ! "

NATURE AND HER CHILD

As some poor child whose soul is windowless,
Having not hearing, speech, nor sight, sits lone
In her dark, silent life, till cometh one
With a most patient heart, who tries to guess

Some hidden way to help her helplessness,
And, yearning for that spirit shut in stone,
A crystal that has never seen the sun,
Smooths now the hair, and now the hand will press,

Or gives a key to touch, then letters raised,
Its symbol; then an apple, or a ring,
And again letters, so, all blind and dumb,
We wait; the kindly smiles of summer come,
And soft winds touch our cheek, and thrushes sing;
The world-heart yearns, but we stand dull and dazed.

THE FOSTER-MOTHER

As some poor Indian woman
  A captive child receives,
And warms it in her bosom,
  And o'er its weeping grieves;

And comforts it with kisses,
  And strives to understand
Its eager, lonely babble,
  Fondling the little hand, —

So Earth, our foster-mother,
  Yearns for us, with her great
Wild heart, and croons in murmurs
  Low, inarticulate.

She knows we are white captives,
  Her dusky race above,
But the deep, childless bosom
  Throbs with its brooding love.

THE LINKS OF CHANCE

HOLDING apoise in air
My twice-dipped pen, — for some tense thread of
    thought
  Had snapped, — mine ears were half aware
Of passing wheels; eyes saw, but mind saw not,
  My sun-shot linden. Suddenly, as I stare,
Two shifting visions grow and fade unsought : —

  Noon-blaze : the broken shade
Of ruins strown. Two Tartar lovers sit
  She gazing on the ground, face turned, afraid;
And he, at her. Silence is all his wit.
  She stoops, picks up a pebble of green jade
To toss; they watch its flight, unheeding it.

  Ages have rolled away;
And round the stone, by chance, if chance there be,
  Sparse soil has caught; a seed, wind-lodged one
    day,
Grown grass; shrubs sprung; at last a tufted tree.
  Lo ! over its snake root yon conquering Bey
Trips backward, fighting — and half Asia free !

TWO VIEWS OF IT

"O WORLD, O glorious world, good-by!"
  Time but to think it — one wild cry
Unuttered, a heart-wrung farewell
To sky and wood and flashing stream,
All gathered in a last swift gleam,
As the crag crumbled, and he fell.

But lo! the thing was wonderful!
After the echoing crash, a lull:
The great fir on the slope below
Had spread its mighty mother-arm,
And caught him, springing like a bow
Of steel, and lowered him safe from harm.

'T was but an instant's dark and daze:
Then, as he felt each limb was sound,
And slowly from the swooning haze
The dizzy trees stood still that whirled,
And the familiar sky and ground,
There grew with them across his brain
A dull regret: "So, world, dark world,
You are come back again!"

TO A FACE AT A CONCERT

WHEN the low music makes a dusk of sound
About us, and the viol or far-off horn
  Swells out above it like a wind forlorn,
  That wanders seeking something never found,
What phantom in your brain, on what dim ground,
  Traces its shadowy lines? What vision, born
  Of unfulfillment, fades in mere self-scorn,
  Or grows, from that still twilight stealing round?
When the lids droop and the hands lie unstrung,
  Dare one divine your dream, while the chords weave
    Their cloudy woof from key to key, and die, —
Is it one fate that, since the world was young,
  Has followed man, and makes him half believe
    The voice of instruments a human cry?

THE THRUSH

THE thrush sings high on the topmost bough, —
Low, louder, low again; and now
He has changed his tree, — you know not how,
   For you saw no flitting wing.

All the notes of the forest-throng,
Flute, reed, and string, are in his song;
Never a fear knows he, nor wrong,
   Nor a doubt of anything.

Small room for care in that soft breast;
All weather that comes is to him the best,
While he sees his mate close on her nest,
   And the woods are full of spring.

He has lost his last year's love, I know, —
He, too, — but 't is little he keeps of woe;
For a bird forgets in a year, and so
   No wonder the thrush can sing.

EVERY-DAY LIFE

THE marble-smith, at his morning task
    Merrily glasses the blue-veined stone,
With stout hands circling smooth. You ask,
    " What will it be, when it is done? "

" A shaft for a young girl's grave." Both hands
    Go back with a will to their sinewy play ;
And he sings like a bird, as he swaying stands,
    A rollicking stave of Love and May.

AT LAST

From all the long, bright daytime's restlessness,
Through starlight's broken promise of redress,
From eyes that care not, hands that cannot bless,
   Down all the wintry, withered, endless train
   Of years that flowered in hope to fruit in pain,
I claim no happiness.

Sweet soul, that art so rich in blessed store,
See all my hungry heart, my need is sore ;
Oh, if thou holdest it, withhold no more !
   Let not that wandering hope, that blind with tears,
   Comes down to me through all the desert years,
Drop dead, even at the door.

What wistful thought thou darest not confess
Shadows thy dawn-lit eyes with tenderness ?
What timid stir as of a mute caress
   Dares only thrill thy trembling finger-tips —
   What word waits, dumb and quivering, at thy lips ?
O Love, my happiness !

FOREST HOME

O Forest-Mother, I have stayed
    Too long away from thee;
Let me come home for these few hours
    That from the world are free.

Oh! mother, they have saddened me
    With all their foolish din;
Lowly I knock at thy green gate;
    Dear mother, let me in.

Down where the tumbled towers of rock
    Their perilous stairs have made,
Holding the tough young hemlock boughs
    For slender balustrade,

I find my pleasant home, far off
    From all men say and do —
Far as the world from which we flash
    When some swift dream breaks through.

Again the grave old hemlock trees
    Stretch down their feathery palms,
And murmur up against the blue
    Their solemn breath of psalms;

And here my little brothers are,
  The sparrow and the bee,
The wren that almost used to dare
  To perch upon my knee;

The dust of sunshine under foot,
  The darkness over head,
The sliding gleam that swings along
  The unseen spider's thread;

The low arched path beneath the boughs,
  And half-way down it laid
A falling fringe of sun-lit leaves
  Against the roof of shade;

The sunshine clasping round both sides
  A broken cedar old,
Rimming its shaft so dark and wet
  In green and massy gold,

In hollows where the evening glooms
  Rest drowsily all day,
In the blue shadows of the pines,
  Sprinkled with golden spray.

Dimpled red cheeks of berries hid
  A wary eye discerns,
And timid little pale-faced flowers
  Peep through the latticed ferns.

O Mother, they are proud and blind
　　Who from all these would stay ;
Yet do not scorn them unforgiven,
　　But woo them day by day.

Let all sweet winds from all fair dells,
　　And whispering breath of pine,
Pursue and lure the wanderer
　　Back to thy rest divine.

If I must build in Babel still
　　Till that last summons come,
Oh ! call me when the hour is near,
　　And let me die at home.

'T were sweet, I know, to stay ; but so
　　'T were sweetest to depart,
Thy cool, still hand upon my face,
　　Thy silence in my heart.

THE SINGER'S CONFESSION

ONCE he cried to all the hills and waters
And the tossing grain and tufted grasses:
" Take my message — tell it to my brothers!
Stricken mute I cannot speak my message.
When the evening wind comes back from ocean,
Singing surf-songs, to Earth's fragrant bosom,
And the beautiful young human creatures
Gather at the mother feet of Nature,
Gazing with their pure and wistful faces,
Tell the old heroic human story.
When they weary of the wheels of science,
Grinding, jangling their harsh dissonances, —
Stones and bones and alkalis and atoms, —
Sing to them of human hope and passion;
And the soul divine, whose incarnation,
Born of love — alas! my message stumbles,
Faints on faltering lips : Oh, speak it for me! "

Then a hush fell; and around about him
Suddenly he felt the mighty shadow
Of the hills, like grave and silent pity;
And, as one who sees without regarding,
The wide wind went over him and left him,
And the brook, repeating low, " His message! "
Babbled, as it fled, a quiet laughter.

What was he, that he had touched their message —
Theirs, who had been chanting it forever :
With whose organ-tones the human spirit
Had eternally been overflowing !
Then, with shame that stung in cheek and forehead,
Slow he crept away.
                    And now he listens,
Mute and still, to hear them tell their message —
All the holy hills and sacred waters ;
When the sea-wind swings its evening censer,
Till the misty incense hides the altar
And the long-robed shadows, lowly kneeling.

A MYTH OF FANTASY AND FIRST LOVE

Hᴉᴅ in the silence of a forest deep
Dwelt a fair soul in flesh that was as fair.
Over her nimble hands her floating hair
Made waving shadows, while her eyes did keep
The winding track of weaving intricate.
Early at morn and at the evening late,
A robe of shimmering silk she wove with care.
Hour after hour, though might she smile or weep,
Still ran the golden or the glooming thread.
Waking she wove that which she dreamed asleep,
Till many a noon had bloomed above her tender head.

Now when the time was full, the robe was done.
Light she would hold it in her loving hand,
And with wide eyes of wonder she would stand
For half the day, and turn it to the sun,
To see its gold lights shift and melt away
And grow again, and flash in myriad play.
Or white it glimmered in each glossy strand,
For half the night she held it to the moon;
Or, sitting with it sleeked across her knee,
She would bend down above it, and would croon
The strangest bits of broken songs that e'er could
        be.

Then came the dawn when (so her doom had said)
Out through the shadowy forest she must go,
And follow whatsoever chance might show,
Or whither any sound her footsteps led;
Taking for wayward guides whatever stirred —
The rustling squirrel, or the startled bird,
Their pathless ways pursuing, fast or slow,
Until the forest's border she should tread.
There whosoever met her, she must fling
That woven wonder blindly on his head,
And see in him her only lord and king.

Dim was the morn, and dew-wet was the way:
Aloft the ancient cedars lifted high
Their jagged crosses on the dawn-streaked sky:
Below, the gossamers were glimmering gray
Along her path, and many a silver thread
Caught glancing lights, in floating curves o'erhead;
And little dew-showers pattered far and nigh,
Where wakened thrushes stirred the sprinkled spray.
For hours she wandered where her footsteps led,
Till a long lance of open sunlight lay
As red as gold upon her lifted, eager head.

Ah, woe for her that mortal doom must be!
Just then the prince came spurring, fair and young,
With heart as merry as the song he sung:
But as she started forward, at her knee
A cringing beggar from the weeds close by

Holds up his cap for alms, with whining cry.
Swift over him the lifted robe was flung:
Henceforth, his slave, forever she must see
All princely beauty in that brutal face —
Heaven send that by some deeper witchery
His swinish soul through her may gain some touch of
       grace.

THE DEPARTURE OF THE PILOT

WRITTEN ON THE DEPARTURE OF PRESIDENT DANIEL C.
GILMAN FROM CALIFORNIA

*Ye university is
likened by ye
poet to a ship.*

SLENDER spars and snowy wings,
　　Arrowy hull that cleaves the foam, —
See! the good ship grandly swings
　　Forth to seek her ocean home.

*She is in peril of
legislatures*

Thro' the narrow harbor-gate,
　　Past the rocks that guard the bay,
Towards where friendlier billows wait,
　　Well she holds her stately way.

and of ye public.

Angry now the breakers are;
　　Gleam their white teeth in the sun,
Where along the shallow bar,
　　Fierce and high their ridges run.

But D. C. G.

But the pilot-captain, lo!
　　How serene in strength is he!
Blithe as winds that dawnward blow,
　　Fresh and fearless as the sea.

Now the shifting breezes fail,
    Baffling gusts arise and die,
Shakes and shudders every sail,   steereth
    Hark! the rocks are roaring nigh.

But the pilot keeps her keel
    Where the current runneth fair,
Deftly turns the massive wheel   her
    Light as though 't were hung in air.

Hark! the bar on either side!
    Hiss of foam, and crash of crest,
Trampling feet, and shouts — they glide   into open water.
    Safely out on ocean's breast.

Then the Pilot gives his hand
    To his brother, close beside:
"Now 't is thine to take command,   He addresseth
    I must back at turn of tide."   J. Le C.

Then the brother-captains true
    Grasp each other by the hand,
Bidding cheerily adieu
    But a moment as they stand.

Something in the elder's eye
    Glimmers — is it but the spray?   And J. Le C.
Something — could it be a sigh,   speaketh
    Or a breeze that died away?   to

And quoth he : " O brother brave,
    Wisely thou hast steered and well,
Now all fair are wind and wave, —
    Come and tarry with us still."

D. C. G.
&

" Wave and wind at last are fair,
    Rosy-bright the new-born day,
Hope and faith are in the air, —
    Come and sail with us for aye ! "

inviteth
him.

But the pilot's shallop-prow
    Chafes against the vessel's side :
" Nay, true heart, thy wisdom now
    Shall the good ship's fortunes guide."

But the overland
locomotive
snorteth

" On the morrow they shall launch
    Yonder from the Eastern shore,
Yet another vessel, staunch,
    Sound as e'er was built before.

and
Johns Hopkins
must be begun.

" Hopes and prayers upon her wait :
    Her deep bosom, grand and free,
Bears a wealth of mystic freight :
    I must guide her to the sea.

" But upon our voyage far
    We shall meet in other days,
Since the same pure polar star
    Shines to beacon both our ways.

But since both
are voyaging
after truth
and progress

" Far away where favoring gales
  Blow from many a spicy beach,
We shall see our shining sails
  Nodding friendly, each to each.

the ships shall
sail in
sight &

" Many a morning that shall dawn
  With its radiant prophecy,
Still shall greet us sailing on —
  Comrades on the glorious sea."

be of ye
same fleet.

Amen.

AN ANSWER

TO THE YALE CLASS OF 1861, READ JUNE 28, 1876

DEAR friends, ask not from me a song:
The singing days to spring belong,
And in our hearts, as in this clime,
Spring has long turned to summer-time.
The morning dreams have fled afar,
When every dew-drop held a star:
The broad, full noon is here — till even
The stars have drawn away to heaven.

With you 't is June; and rosebuds blush,
And golden sunsets glow and flush:
While every breeze, with Psyche wings,
Wafts promise of immortal things;
And every shower of perfumed rain
Brightens to rainbow hope again.
'T is meet that in that fragrant air
Your songs defy old Time and care,
While overhead the elms shall swing,
And hand to hand old friendships cling:
Ah, sweet and strong your voices ring!

But here, upon the planet's verge,
The grassy velvet turns to serge:
No shower has wet the hillocks sere
Since April shed her parting tear.
The poppies on the hill are dead,
And the wild oat is harvested:
The canyon's flowers are brown with seed,
And only blooms some wayside weed.
No leafy elms their shadows throw,
No moist and odorous breezes blow;
But all the bare, brown hills along
The ocean wind sweeps sad and strong.
Then ask not, friends, from me a song!

Yet think not that this sombre strain
Would, dear old friends, of fate complain.
Though spring has gone, and singing days,
The sunshine, and the starshine, stays.
If no more bloom the hillsides yield,
The tented sheaves are in the field:
The tawny slopes are sending down
Their harvest loads to farm and town.
If early spring-time fled with tears,
Yet earlier harvest-time appears.
And if far off, as in a dream,
I see your merry faces beam,
And if far off, as through the deep,
I hear your songs their cadence keep,
I know 't were childishness to weep.

For all the time is grand indeed!
And whether June bring flower or seed —
And whether softest breezes blow,
Or ocean's organ-music flow,
Not backward only turn our eyes,
But forward, where along the skies
The brighter dawn-lights break and rise.
For all the love these years have stored
Wells up to manlier deed and word.
The nerveless grasp of girlish youth
Grips now the banner staff of truth;
The careless song, half sung, rings out
Changed to a mighty battle-shout;
And we that kept our holiday
With wine and fragrant mists and play,
Shall yet, perchance, even such as we,
Fulfill our half-heard prophecy.
The vision we but half divined,
Wrought out with steadier heart and mind,
Shall bless the world of humankind.

IN MEMORY OF A MUSICIAN

DIED SAN FRANCISCO, OCTOBER, 1878

DEAD! And the echoes dumb,
That thrilled our very inmost soul to hear:
And now through all the rich autumnal air,
    His city's hum
Murmurs in fitful throbs, like dying beat
    Of funeral drum!

Hark! 't is the voice of song —
No dirge, no requiem chant of hopeless woe,
With tramp of dull, unwilling footsteps slow:
    Nay, that would wrong
The cheery life that ever was so sweet,
    Tender and strong:

But waves along the shore,
That plash and sing like little children's mirth,
Whose faces he loved best of all the earth,
    And winds that o'er
This lonely world still blow, never to greet
    His music more —

Those waves and winds I hear,
And whispering trees, and note of happy bird,

And Nature's every mellow tone is heard,
    Singing full clear
The old immortal harmonies his feet
    Followed so near.

    Still, Nature, still repeat
Thy purest symphonies for his pure sake,
Whose heart love's grandest victory could take
    From love's defeat;
Whose life was bruised, like some sweet herb, to
    make
    All others sweet.

A DREAM WITHIN A DREAM

YALE CLUB, SAN FRANCISCO, DECEMBER 12, 1878

THE green was all with shadows blent;
  The night-wind, surf-like, here and there
Broke softly on the elms and sent
  Its spray of whispers down the air.

The empty streets, long silent, hid
  Beneath their leafy arches lay:
Only a sleepy cricket chid,
  Or distant footfall died away.

Our college feast had broken up;
  No banquet rich, no spices rare,
No gleam of wine from jeweled cup,
  But youth, immortal youth was there.

'T was boyish talk, — the race crew's fate,
  The jovial tutor's joke and grin,
And who would conquer in debate,
  And who would wear the mystic pin.

No clutching Past our spirits held:
  Our eyes looked forward; it was spring:
The fresh sap stirred, the new buds swelled —
  No wonder we could feast and sing.

The small puns crackled, and ere long
   The deeper thoughts would come and go;
And evermore some burst of song
   Startled the slumbering rooms below.

And when we parted — not too soon —
   With shouted calls from mate to mate,
We laughed to see the tipsy moon
   Rise staring, crooked-faced, so late.

We strolled, my friend and I, to where
   The street becomes a wooded lane:
Talking of many a fancy fair,
   And all the blossoms of the brain.

Our life should break, we said, its bars
   And we would sail the seas, and there
Beneath that western crown of stars
   The golden future we would share.

The sleepy elms were breathing low,
   Phantoms their hollow arches filled;
The withered moon lay faint and low;
   Fantastic shadows stirred and stilled.

But on I wandered, now alone,
   And where the wooded lane grew steep
Sat drowsing: the weird dark had grown
   A part of me; I seemed to sleep.

And all the present years were dead —
    Their stormy joys, their passions sweet;
And youth and wingèd hope were fled
    Adown the dark with silent feet.

The night wind seemed more chill to be;
    The hills rose strangely bare and round:
A great bay narrowed to the sea
    Beyond the city's glimmering mound.

My brain was numb, my heart was lead;
    Dear faces faded far and cold;
Some were forgotten, some were dead,
    And all were scattered, chill, and old.

That feast night 'mid the floating trees
    Seemed ages in the silent past;
Those friendships, darling memories, —
    Too pure, too warm, too sweet to last.

Among the hillslopes, wan and sad,
    The marbles of a graveyard gleamed,
And ghosts were near, and I was glad
    Even in my dream to think I dreamed.

But still I thought I dreamed : the west
    Grew gray, and troops of fog came in,
Stalking across the city's crest
    Like ghastly shapes of joy and sin.

The white dawn seemed to grow more cold;
Its bitter breath was freezing me:
I shivered, and awoke — behold!
The bare, round hills, the muffled sea.

The mountain peak beyond the bay,
Stern, silent, as the vanquished are;
Round him the folded shadows lay,
And on his forehead was a scar.

The vision I had found so drear
Waked with me, and is with me still;
The future of my dream was here,
And I had slept on Berkeley hill.

I had arisen before unclosed
The sleeping orient's earliest gleam,
And climbed, and sat, or mused and dozed,
And dreamed this dream within a dream.

But now the full dawn comes: the sun
Breaks through the canyon with his gold,
The jocund lark-songs have begun,
The mountain's brow is clear and bold.

The good salt sea wind blows; the mist
Unveils the city shining fair;
Its floating shreds the sun has kissed
To pearls that fleck the upper air.

So drift away the moods of night,
　So shines the manlier purpose free;
The breezy Present wakes in light,
　And plans the richer world to be.

A RESTING-PLACE

A SEA of shade; with hollow heights above,
   Where floats the redwood's airy roof away,
Whose feathery lace the drowsy breezes move,
   And softly through the azure windows play:
   No nearer stir than yon white cloud astray,
No closer sound than sob of distant dove.

I only live as the deep forest's swoon
   Dreams me amid its dream; for all things fade
Nor pulse of mine disturbs the unconscious noon.
   Even love and hope are still — albeit they made
   My heart beat yesterday — in slumber laid,
Like yon dim ghost that last night was the moon.

Only the bending grass, grown gray and sere,
   Nods now and then, where at my feet it swings,
Pleased that another like itself is here,
   Unseen among the mighty forest things —
   Another fruitless life, that fading clings
To earth and autumn days in doubt and fear.

Dream on, O wood! O wind, stay in thy west,
   Nor wake the shadowy spirit of the fern,

Asleep along the fallen pine-tree's breast!
  That, till the sun go down, and night-stars burn,
  And the chill dawn-breath from the sea return,
Tired earth may taste heaven's honey-dew of rest.

THE MYSTERY

I NEVER know why 't is I love thee so:
   I do not think 't is that thine eyes for me
   Grow bright as sudden sunshine on the sea;
Nor for thy rose-leaf lips, or breast of snow,
Or voice like quiet waters where they flow.

So why I love thee well I cannot tell:
   Only it is that when thou speak'st to me
   'T is thy voice speaks, and when thy face I see
It is thy face I see; and it befell
Thou wert, and I was, and I love thee well.

THE FOOL'S PRAYER

THE royal feast was done; the King
  Sought some new sport to banish care,
And to his jester cried: " Sir Fool,
  Kneel now, and make for us a prayer!"

The jester doffed his cap and bells,
  And stood the mocking court before;
They could not see the bitter smile
  Behind the painted grin he wore.

He bowed his head, and bent his knee
  Upon the monarch's silken stool;
His pleading voice arose: " O Lord,
  Be merciful to me, a fool!

" No pity, Lord, could change the heart
  From red with wrong to white as wool;
The rod must heal the sin: but, Lord,
  Be merciful to me, a fool!

" 'T is not by guilt the onward sweep
  Of truth and right, O Lord, we stay;
'T is by our follies that so long
  We hold the earth from heaven away.

" These clumsy feet, still in the mire,
 Go crushing blossoms without end;
These hard, well-meaning hands we thrust
 Among the heart-strings of a friend.

" The ill-timed truth we might have kept —
 Who knows how sharp it pierced and stung?
The word we had not sense to say —
 Who knows how grandly it had rung?

" Our faults no tenderness should ask,
 The chastening stripes must cleanse them all;
But for our blunders — oh, in shame
 Before the eyes of heaven we fall.

" Earth bears no balsam for mistakes;
 Men crown the knave, and scourge the tool
That did his will; but Thou, O Lord,
 Be merciful to me, a fool! "

The room was hushed; in silence rose
 The King, and sought his gardens cool,
And walked apart, and murmured low,
 " Be merciful to me, a fool! "

OPPORTUNITY

This I beheld, or dreamed it in a dream : —
There spread a cloud of dust along a plain ;
And underneath the cloud, or in it, raged
A furious battle, and men yelled, and swords
Shocked upon swords and shields. A prince's banner
Wavered, then staggered backward, hemmed by foes.
A craven hung along the battle's edge,
And thought, " Had I a sword of keener steel —
That blue blade that the king's son bears, — but this
Blunt thing — ! " he snapt and flung it from his hand,
And lowering crept away and left the field.
Then came the king's son, wounded, sore bestead,
And weaponless, and saw the broken sword,
Hilt-buried in the dry and trodden sand,
And ran and snatched it, and with battle-shout
Lifted afresh he hewed his enemy down,
And saved a great cause that heroic day.

AN ASPIRATION

YALE CLUB, SAN FRANCISCO, DECEMBER 11, 1879

LET us return once more, we said,
And greet the saintly mother Yale;
That gray and venerable head,
That wrinkled brow, time-worn and pale.

So from afar we fared, and found
Her children thronging round her feet:
The summer all her elms had crowned,
The dappled grass was cool and sweet.

But lo! no ancient dame was there,
With tottering step and waning powers:
Our maiden mother, fresh and fair,
Stood queenlike 'mid her trees and towers.

Men may grow old: Time's tremulous hands
Still hasten the spent glass; but she —
" Mewing her mighty youth " she stands,
And wears her laurels royally.

From olden fountain-wells that flow
Down every sacred height of truth,
As pure as fire, as cold as snow,
Her lips have quaffed immortal youth.

Her feet in fields of amaranth tread,
  Lilies of every golden clime
Are in her hand, and round her head
  The aureole of the coming time.

Ah, maiden-mother, might there rise
  On these far shores a power like thine,
With Learning's sceptre, mild and wise,
  And all the sister Arts benign !

It matters little that it bear
  The name that Cloyne's great bishop bore,
If only it might bring the fair
  Fulfillment of his thought of yore;

If somewhere, on the hill or plain,
  By forest's calm, or quickening sea,
Or where the town's electric brain
  With silent lightnings flashes free, —

If one like Yale among us stood,
  To nourish at her ample breast
And feed with her ambrosial food
  The infant vigor of the West.

The smitten rocks pour forth in vain
  Their Midas-streams : when shall be wrought
From out our store some classic fane,
  Some cloistered home of finer thought ?

Ofttimes a troubled mood will bring
 The vision of a land forlorn,
Where gold is prophet, priest, and king,
 And wisdom is a name of scorn;

Whose treasures build the gambler's halls,
 Whose tinsel follies flaunt the skies,
Whose horses feed in marble stalls,
 While Learning begs for crumbs, and dies.

The waves that throb from Asia's breast
 Prophetic murmur on our shore:
Barbarian throngs from East, from West —
 Who knows what fortunes are in store?

Nay, thou foreboding mood, be still!
 And let a farther-sighted pen
Point out the better fate that Will
 And Hope make possible to men.

What man has done, still man can do:
 Of slumbering force there is no dearth;
And beckoning hands and hearts may woo
 The banished Muses back to earth.

We, too, those fountain-wells have known,
 And quaffed the life no years destroy;
And under every snowiest crown
 Still dreams and yearns the immortal Boy.

Nor shall that yearning be in vain :
  With boyish hope but manlier will
We dream our rosy dreams again,
  And build our airy castles still.

But not of passion's luring wraith,
  Nor selfish fancy's empty foam ;
Of steadfast brother-love, in faith,
  We build the better time to come.

THE NORTH WIND

ALL night, beneath the flashing hosts of stars,
The North poured forth the passion of its soul
In mighty longings for the tawny South,
Sleeping afar among her orange-blooms.
All night, through the deep cañon's organ-pipes,
Swept down the grand orchestral harmonies
Tumultuous, till the hills' rock buttresses
Trembled in unison.

           The sun has risen,
But still the storming sea of air beats on,
And o'er the broad green slopes a flood of light
Comes streaming through the heavens like a wind,
Till every leaf and twig becomes a lyre
And thrills with vibrant splendor.

              Down the bay
The furrowed blue, save that 't is starred with foam,
Is bare and empty as the sky of clouds;
For all the little sails, that yesterday
Flocked past the islands, now have furled their wings,
And huddled frightened at the wharves — just as,
A moment since, a flock of twittering birds
Whirled through the almond-trees like scattered leaves,
And hid beyond the hedge.

                    How the old oaks
Stand stiffly to it, and wrestle with the storm!
While the tall eucalyptus' plumy tops
Tumble and toss and stream with quivering light.
Hark! when it lulls a moment at the ear,
The fir-trees sing their sea-song: — now again
The roar is all about us like a flood;
And like a flood the fierce light shines, and burns
Away all distance, till the far blue ridge,
That rims the ocean, rises close at hand,
And high, Prometheus-like, great Tamalpais
Lifts proudly his grand front, and bears his scar,
Heaven's scath of wrath, defiant like a god.

I thank thee, glorious wind! Thou bringest me
Something that breathes of mountain crags and pines,
Yea, more — from the unsullied, farthest North,
Where crashing icebergs jar like thunder shocks,
And midnight splendors wave and fade and flame,
Thou bring'st a keen, fierce joy. So wilt thou help
The soul to rise in strength, as some great wave
Leaps forth, and shouts, and lifts the ocean-foam,
And rides exultant round the shining world.

THE TREE OF MY LIFE

WHEN I was yet but a child, the gardener gave me a
tree,
A little slim elm, to be set wherever seemed good to
me.
What a wonderful thing it seemed! with its lace-edge
leaves uncurled,
And its span-long stem, that should grow to the grandest tree in the world!
So I searched all the garden round, and out over field
and hill,
But not a spot could I find that suited my wayward
will.
I would have it bowered in the grove, in a close and
quiet vale;
I would rear it aloft on the height, to wrestle with the
gale.

Then I said, " I will cover its roots with a little earth
by the door,
And there it shall live and wait, while I search for a
place once more."
But still I could never find it, the place for my wondrous tree,
And it waited and grew by the door, while years
passed over me;

Till suddenly, one fine day, I saw it was grown too
  tall,
And its roots gone down too deep, to be ever moved
  at all.

So here it is growing still, by the lowly cottage door;
Never so grand and tall as I dreamed it would be of
  yore,
But it shelters a tired old man in its sunshine-dappled
  shade,
The children's pattering feet round its knotty knees
  have played,
Dear singing birds in a storm sometimes take refuge
  there,
And the stars through its silent boughs shine glori-
  ously fair.

THE DESERTER

Blindest and most frantic prayer,
　　Clutching at a senseless boon,
His that begs, in mad despair,
　　Death to come; — he comes so soon!

Like a reveler that strains
　　Lip and throat to drink it up —
The last ruby that remains,
　　One red droplet in the cup,

Like a child that, sullen, mute,
　　Sulking spurns, with chin on breast,
Of the Tree of Life a fruit,
　　His gift of whom he is the guest,

Outcast on the thither shore,
　　Open scorn to him shall give
Souls that heavier burdens bore :
　　" See the wretch that dared not live ! "

A CALIFORNIAN'S DREAMS

A THUNDER-STORM of the olden days!
The red sun sinks in a sleepy haze;
The sultry twilight, close and still,
Muffles the cricket's drowsy trill.
Then a round-topped cloud rolls up the west,
Black to its smouldering, ashy crest,
And the chariot of the storm you hear,
With its jarring axle rumbling near;
Till the blue is hid, and here and there
The sudden, blinding lightnings glare.
Scattering now the big drops fall,
Till the rushing rain in a silver wall
Blurs the line of the bending elms,
Then blots them out and the landscape whelms.
A flash — a clap, and a rumbling peal:
The broken clouds the blue reveal;
The last bright drops fall far away,
And the wind, that had slept for heat all day,
With a long-drawn sigh awakes again
And drinks the cool of the blessed rain.

November! night, and a sleety storm:
Close are the ruddy curtains, warm
And rich in the glow of the roaring grate,

It may howl outside like a baffled fate,
And rage on the roof, and lash the pane
With its fierce and impotent wrath in vain.
Sitting within at our royal ease
We sing to the chime of the ivory keys,
And feast our hearts from script and score
With the wealth of the mellow hearts of yore.

A winter's night on a world of snow!
Not a sound above, not a stir below ·
The moon hangs white in the icy air,
And the shadows are motionless everywhere.
Is this the planet that we know ––
This silent floor of the ghostly snow?
Or is this the moon, so still and dead,
And yonder orb far overhead,
With its silver map of plain and sea,
Is that the earth where we used to be?
Shall we float away in the frosty blue
To that living, summer world we knew,
With its full, hot heart-beats as of old,
Or be frozen phantoms of the cold?

A river of ice, all blue and glare,
Under a star-shine dim and rare.
The sheeny sheet in the sparkling light
Is ribbed with slender wisps of white ––
Crinkles of snow, that the flying steel
Lightly crunches with ringing heel.

Swinging swift as the swallows skim,
You round the shadowy river's rim:
Falling somewhere out of the sky
Hollow and weird is the owlet's cry;
The gloaming woods seem phantom hosts,
And the bushes cower in the snow like ghosts.
Till the tinkling feet that with you glide
Skate closer and closer to your side,
And something steals from a furry muff,
And you clasp it and cannot wonder enough
That a little palm so soft and fair
Could keep so warm in the frosty air.

'T is thus we dream in our tranquil clime,
Rooted still in the olden time;
Longing for all those glooms and gleams
Of passionate Nature's mad extremes.
Or was it only our hearts, that swelled
With the youth and life and love they held?

THE VENUS OF MILO, AND OTHER POEMS

THE VENUS OF MILO

THERE fell a vision to Praxiteles:
Watching thro' drowsy lids the loitering seas
That lay caressing with white arms of foam
The sleeping marge of his Ionian home.
He saw great Aphrodite standing near,
Knew her, at last, the Beautiful he had sought
With lifelong passion, and in love and fear
Into unsullied stone the vision wrought.

Far other was the form that Cnidos gave
To senile Rome, no longer free or brave, —
The Medicean, naked like a slave.
The Cnidians built her shrine
Of creamy ivory fine;
Most costly was the floor
Of scented cedar, and from door
Was looped to carven door
Rich stuff of Tyrian purple, in whose shade
Her glistening shoulders and round limbs outshone,

Milk-white as lilies in a summer moon.
Here honey-hearted Greece to worship came,
And on her altar leaped a turbid flame.
The quickened blood ran dancing to its doom,
And lip sought trembling lip in that rich gloom.

But the island people of Cos, by the salt main
From Persia's touch kept clean,
Chose for their purer shrine amid the seas
That grander vision of Praxiteles.
Long ages after, sunken in the ground
Of sea-girt Melos, wondering shepherds found
The marred and dinted copy which men name
Venus of Milo, saved to endless fame.

Before the broken marble, on a day,
There came a worshiper : a slanted ray
Struck in across the dimness of her shrine
And touched her face as to a smile divine;
For it was like the worship of a Greek
At her old altar. Thus I heard him speak : —

Men call thee Love : is there no holier name
Than hers, the foam-born, laughter-loving dame ?
Nay, for there is than love no holier name :
All words that pass the lips of mortal men
With inner and with outer meaning shine;
An outer gleam that meets the common ken,
An inner light that but the few divine.

Thou art the love celestial, seeking still
The soul beneath the form; the serene will;
The wisdom, of whose deeps the sages dream;
The unseen beauty that doth faintly gleam
In stars, and flowers, and waters where they roll;
The unheard music whose faint echoes even
Make whosoever hears a homesick soul
Thereafter, till he follow it to heaven.

Larger than mortal woman I see thee stand,
With beautiful head bent forward steadily,
As if those earnest eyes could see
Some glorious thing far off, to which thy hand
Invisibly stretched onward seems to be.
From thy white forehead's breadth of calm, the
      hair
Sweeps lightly, as a cloud in windless air.
Placid thy brows, as that still line at dawn
Where the dim hills along the sky are drawn,
When the last stars are drowned in deeps afar.
Thy quiet mouth — I know not if it smile,
Or if in some wise pity thou wilt weep, —
Little as one may tell, some summer morn,
Whether the dreamy brightness is most glad,
Or wonderfully sad, —
So bright, so still thy lips serenely sleep;
So fixedly thine earnest eyes the while,
As clear and steady as the morning star,
Their gaze upon that coming glory keep.

Thy garment's fallen folds
Leave beautiful the fair, round breast
In sacred loveliness; the bosom deep
Where happy babe might sleep;
The ample waist no narrowing girdle holds,
Where daughters slim might come to cling and rest,
Like tendriled vines against the plane-tree pressed.
Around thy firm, large limbs and steady feet
The robes slope downward, as the folded hills
Slope round the mountain's knees, when shadow fills
The hollow cañons, and the wind is sweet
From russet oat-fields and the ripening wheat.

From our low world no gods have taken wing;
Even now upon our hills the twain are wandering:
The Medicean's sly and servile grace,
And the immortal beauty of thy face.
One is the spirit of all short-lived love
And outward, earthly loveliness:
The tremulous rosy morn is her mouth's smile,
The sky her laughing azure eyes above;
And, waiting for caress,
Lie bare the soft hill-slopes, the while
Her thrilling voice is heard
In song of wind and wave, and every flitting bird.
Not plainly, never quite herself she shows;
Just a swift glance of her illumined smile
Along the landscape goes;
Just a soft hint of singing, to beguile

A man from all his toil;
Some vanished gleam of beckoning arm, to spoil
A morning's task with longing wild and vain.
Then if across the parching plain
He seek her, she with passion burns
His heart to fever, and he hears
The west wind's mocking laughter when he turns,
Shivering in mist of ocean's sullen tears.
It is the Medicean: well I know
The arts her ancient subtlety will show;
The stubble-fields she turns to ruddy gold;
The empty distance she will fold
In purple gauze; the warm glow she has kissed
Along the chilling mist:
Cheating and cheated love that grows to hate
And ever deeper loathing, soon or late.

Thou, too, O fairer spirit, walkest here
Upon the lifted hills:
Wherever that still thought within the breast
The inner beauty of the world hath moved;
In starlight that the dome of evening fills;
On endless waters rounding to the west:
For them who thro' that beauty's veil have loved
The soul of all things beautiful the best.
For lying broad awake, long ere the dawn,
Staring against the dark, the blank of space
Opens immeasurably, and thy face
Wavers and glimmers there and is withdrawn.

And many days, when all one's work is vain,
And life goes stretching on, a waste gray plain,
With even the short mirage of morning gone,
No cool breath anywhere, no shadow nigh
Where a weary man might lay him down and die,
Lo! thou art there before me suddenly,
With shade as if a summer cloud did pass,
And spray of fountains whispering to the grass.
Oh, save me from the haste and noise and heat
That spoil life's music sweet:
And from that lesser Aphrodite there —
Even now she stands
Close as I turn, and, O my soul, how fair!
Nay, I will heed not thy white beckoning hands,
Nor thy soft lips like the curled inner leaf
In a rosebud's breast, kissed languid by the sun,
Nor eyes like liquid gleams where waters run.
Yea, thou art beautiful as morn;
And even as I draw nigh
To scoff, I own the loveliness I scorn.
Farewell, for thou hast lost me: keep thy train
Of worshipers; me thou dost lure in vain:
The inner passion, pure as very fire,
Burns to light ash the earthlier desire.

O greater Aphrodite, unto thee
Let me not say farewell. What would Earth be
Without thy presence? Surely unto me
A lifelong weariness, a dull, bad dream.

Abide with me, and let thy calm brows beam
Fresh hope upon me every amber dawn,
New peace when evening's violet veil is drawn.
Then, tho' I see along the glooming plain
The Medicean's waving hand again,
And white feet glimmering in the harvest-field,
I shall not turn, nor yield;
But as heaven deepens, and the Cross and Lyre
Lift up their stars beneath the Northern Crown,
Unto the yearning of the world's desire
I shall be 'ware of answer coming down;
And something, when my heart the darkness stills,
Shall tell me, without sound or any sight,
That other footsteps are upon the hills;
Till the dim earth is luminous with the light
Of the white dawn, from some far-hidden shore,
That shines upon thy forehead evermore.

FIELD NOTES[1]

I

By the wild fence-row, all grown up
With tall oats, and the buttercup,
And the seeded grass, and blue flax-flower,
I fling myself in a nest of green,
Walled about and all unseen,
And lose myself in the quiet hour.
Now and then from the orchard-tree
To the sweet clover at my knee
Hums the crescendo of a bee,
Making the silence seem more still;
Overhead on a maple prong
The least of birds, a jeweled sprite,
With burnished throat and needle bill,
Wags his head in the golden light,
Till it flashes, and dulls, and flashes bright,
Cheeping his microscopic song.

II

Far up the hill-farm, where the breeze
Dips its wing in the billowy grain,
Waves go chasing from the plain
On softly undulating seas;
Now near my nest they swerve and turn,

[1] Written for the graduating class of 1882, at Smith College, North-
ampton, Mass.

And now go wandering without aim;
Or yonder, where the poppies burn,
Race up the slope in harmless flame.
Sometimes the bold wind sways my walls,
My four green walls of the grass and oats,
But never a slender column falls,
And the blue sky-roof above them floats.
Cool in the glowing sun I feel
On wrist and cheek the sea-breeze steal
From the wholesome ocean brine.
The air is full of the whispering pine,
Surf-sound of an aerial sea;
And the light clashing, near and far,
As of mimic shield and scimitar,
Of the slim Australian tree.

III

So all that azure day
In the lap of the green world I lay;
And drinking of the sunshine's flood,
Like Sigurd when the dragon's blood
Made the bird-songs understood,
Inward or outward I could hear
A murmuring of music near;
And this is what it seemed to say : —

IV

Old earth, how beautiful thou art!
Though restless fancy wander wide

And sigh in dreams for spheres more blest,
Save for some trouble, half-confessed,
Some least misgiving, all my heart
With such a world were satisfied.
Had every day such skies of blue,
Were men all wise, and women true,
Might youth as calm as manhood be,
And might calm manhood keep its lore
And still be young — and one thing more,
Old earth were fair enough for me.

Ah, sturdy world, old patient world!
Thou hast seen many times and men;
Heard jibes and curses at thee hurled
From cynic lip and peevish pen.
But give the mother once her due:
· Were women wise, and men all true —
And one thing more that may not be,
Old earth were fair enough for me.

v

If only we were worthier found
Of the stout ball that bears us round!
New wants, new ways, pert plans of change,
New answers to old questions strange;
But to the older questions still
No new replies have come, or will.
New speed to buzz abroad and see
Cities where one needs not to be;

But no new way to dwell at home,
Or there to make great friendships come ;
No novel way to seek or find
True hearts and the heroic mind.
Of atom force and chemic stew
Nor Socrates nor Cæsar knew,
But the old ages knew a plan —
The lost art — how to mould a man.

VI

World, wise old world,
What may man do for thee?
Thou that art greater than all of us,
What wilt thou do to me?
This glossy curve of the tall grass-spear —
Can I make its lustrous green more clear?
This tapering shaft of oat, that knows
To grow erect as the great pine grows,
And to sway in the wind as well as he —
Can I teach it to nod more graciously?
The lark on the mossy rail so nigh,
Wary, but pleased if I keep my place —
Who could give a single grace
To his flute-note sweet and high,
Or help him find his nest hard by?
Can I add to the poppy's gold one bit?
Can I deepen the sky, or soften it?

VII

Æons ago a rock crashed down
From a mountain's crown,
Where a tempest's tread
Crumbled it from its hold.
Ages dawn and in turn grow old:
The rock lies still and dead.
Flames come and floods come,
Sea rolls this mountain crumb
To a pebble, in its play;
Till at the last man came to be,
And a thousand generations passed away.
Then from the bed of a brook one day
A boy with the heart of a king
Fitted the stone to his shepherd sling,
And a giant fell, and a royal race was free.
Not out of any cloud or sky
Will thy good come to prayer or cry.
Let the great forces, wise of old,
Have their whole way with thee,
Crumble thy heart from its hold,
Drown thy life in the sea.
And æons hence, some day,
The love thou gavest a child,
The dream in a midnight wild,
The word thou wouldst not say —
Or in a whisper no one dared to hear,
Shall gladden the earth and bring the golden year.

VIII

Just now a spark of fire
Flashed from a builder's saw
On the ribs of a roof a mile away.
His has been the better day,
Gone not in dreams, nor even the subtle desire
Not to desire;
But work is the sober law
He knows well to obey.
It is a poem he fits and fashions well;
And the five chambers are five acts of it:
Hope in one shall dwell,
In another fear will sit;
In the chamber on the east
Shall be the bridal feast;
In the western one
The dead shall lie alone.
So the cycles of life shall fill
The clean, pine-scented rooms where now he works
    his will.

IX

Might one be healed from fevering thought,
And only look, each night,
On some plain work well wrought,
Or if a man as right and true might be
As a flower or tree!
I would give up all the mind

In the prim city's hoard can find —
House with its scrap-art bedight,
Straitened manners of the street,
Smooth-voiced society —
If so the swiftness of the wind
Might pass into my feet;
If so the sweetness of the wheat
Into my soul might pass,
And the clear courage of the grass;
If the lark caroled in my song;
If one tithe of the faithfulness
Of the bird-mother with her brood
Into my selfish heart might press,
And make me also instinct-good.

X

Life is a game the soul can play
With fewer pieces than men say.
Only to grow as the grass grows,
Prating not of joys or woes;
To burn as the steady hearth-fire burns;
To shine as the star can shine,
Or only as the mote of dust that turns
Darkling and twinkling in the beam of light divine;
And for my wisdom — glad to know
Where the sweetest beech-nuts grow,
And to track out the spicy root,
Or peel the musky core of the wild-berry shoot;
And how the russet ground-bird bold

With both slim feet at once will lightly rake the
     mould;
And why moon-shadows from the swaying limb
Here are sharp and there are dim;
And how the ant his zigzag way can hold
Through the grass that is a grove to him.

'T were good to live one's life alone.
So to share life with many a one:
To keep a thought seven years, and then
Welcome it coming to you
On the way from another's brain and pen,
So to judge if it be true.
Then would the world be fair,
Beautiful as is the past,
Whose beauty we can see at last,
Since self no more is there.

XI

I will be glad to be and do,
And glad of all good men that live,
For they are woof of nature too;
Glad of the poets every one,
Pure Longfellow, great Emerson,
And all that Shakespeare's world can give.
When the road is dust, and the grass dries,
Then will I gaze on the deep skies;
And if Dame Nature frown in cloud,
Well, mother — then my heart shall say —

You cannot so drive me away;
I will still exult aloud,
Companioned of the good hard ground,
Whereon stout hearts of every clime,
In the battles of all time,
Foothold and couch have found.

XII

Joy to the laughing troop
That from the threshold starts,
Led on by courage and immortal hope,
And with the morning in their hearts.
They to the disappointed earth shall give
The lives we meant to live,
Beautiful, free, and strong;
The light we almost had
Shall make them glad;
The words we waited long
Shall run in music from their voice and song.
Unto our world hope's daily oracles
From their lips shall be brought;
And in our lives love's hourly miracles
By them be wrought.
Their merry task shall be
To make the house all fine and sweet
Its new inhabitants to greet,
The wondrous dawning century.

XIII

And now the close of this fair day was come;
The bay grew duskier on its purple floor,
And the long curve of foam
Drew its white net along a dimmer shore.
Through the fading saffron light,
Through the deepening shade of even,
The round earth rolled into the summer night,
And watched the kindling of the stars in heaven.

CALIFORNIA WINTER

This is not winter: where is the crisp air,
And snow upon the roof, and frozen ponds,
And the star-fire that tips the icicle?

Here blooms the late rose, pale and odorless;
And the vague fragrance in the garden walks
Is but a doubtful dream of mignonette.
In some smooth spot, under a sleeping oak
That has not dreamed of such a thing as spring,
The ground has stolen a kiss from the cool sun
And thrilled a little, and the tender grass
Has sprung untimely, for these great bright days,
Staring upon it, will not let it live.
The sky is blue, and 't is a goodly time,
And the round, barren hillsides tempt the feet;
But 't is not winter: such as seems to man
What June is to the roses, sending floods
Of life and color through the tingling veins.

It is a land without a fireside. Far
Is the old home, where, even this very night,
Roars the great chimney with its glorious fire,
And old friends look into each other's eyes
Quietly, for each knows the other's trust.

Heaven is not far away such winter nights:
The big white stars are sparkling in the east,
And glitter in the gaze of solemn eyes;
For many things have faded with the flowers,
And many things their resurrection wait;
Earth like a sepulchre is sealed with frost,
And Morn and Even beside the silent door
Sit watching, and their soft and folded wings
Are white with feathery snow.

                                    Yet even here
We are not quite forgotten by the Hours,
Could human eyes but see the beautiful
Save through the glamour of a memory.
Soon comes the strong south wind, and shouts aloud
Its jubilant anthem. Soon the singing rain
Comes from warm seas, and in its skyey tent
Enwraps the drowsy world. And when, some night,
Its flowing folds invisibly withdraw,
Lo! the new life in all created things!
The azure mountains and the ocean gates
Against the lovely sky stand clean and clear
As a new purpose in the wiser soul.

THE LOVER'S SONG

Lend me thy fillet, Love!
  I would no longer see;
Cover mine eyelids close awhile,
  And·make me blind like thee.

Then might I pass her sunny face,
  And know not it was fair;
Then might I hear her voice, nor guess
  Her starry eyes were there.

Ah! banished so from stars and sun —
  Why need it be my fate?
If only she might deem me good
  And wise, and be my mate!

Lend her thy fillet, Love!
  Let her no longer see:
If there is hope for me at all,
  She must be blind like thee.

RECALL

"Love me, or I am slain!" I cried, and meant
Bitterly true each word. Nights, morns, slipped by,
Moons, circling suns, yet still alive am I;
But shame to me, if my best time be spent

On this perverse, blind passion! Are we sent
Upon a planet just to mate and die,
A man no more than some pale butterfly
That yields his day to nature's sole intent?

Or is my life but Marguerite's ox-eyed flower,
That I should stand and pluck and fling away,
One after one, the petal of each hour,
Like a love-dreamy girl, and only say,
"Loves me," and "loves me not," and "loves me"?
        Nay!
Let the man's mind awake to manhood's power.

THE REFORMER

BEFORE the monstrous wrong he sets him down —
One man against a stone-walled city of sin.
For centuries those walls have been a-building;
Smooth porphyry, they slope and coldly glass
The flying storm and wheeling sun. No chink,
No crevice lets the thinnest arrow in.
He fights alone, and from the cloudy ramparts
A thousand evil faces gibe and jeer him.
Let him lie down and die : what is the right,
And where is justice, in a world like this ?
But by and by, earth shakes herself, impatient ;
And down, in one great roar of ruin, crash
Watch-tower and citadel and battlements.
When the red dust has cleared, the lonely soldier
Stands with strange thoughts beneath the friendly
      stars.

DESIRE OF SLEEP

It is not death I mean,
  Nor even forgetfulness,
But healthful human sleep,
Dreamless, and still, and deep,
  Where I would hide and glean
    Some heavenly balm to bless.

I would not die; I long
  To live, to see my days
Bud once again, and bloom,
And make amidst them room
  For thoughts like birds of song,
    Out-winging happy ways.

I would not even forget:
  Only, a little while —
Just now — I cannot bear
Remembrance with despair;
  The years are coming yet
    When I shall look, and smile.

Not now — oh, not to-night!
  Too clear on midnight's deep

Come voice and hand and touch;
The heart aches overmuch —
   Hush sounds! shut out the light!
   A little I *must* sleep.

EVE'S DAUGHTER

I WAITED in the little sunny room:
    The cool breeze waved the window-lace, at play,
The white rose on the porch was all in bloom,
    And out upon the bay
I watched the wheeling sea-birds go and come.

"Such an old friend, — she would not make me stay
    While she bound up her hair." I turned, and lo,
Danaë in her shower! and fit to slay
    All a man's hoarded prudence at a blow:
Gold hair, that streamed away
    As round some nymph a sunlit fountain's flow.
"She would not make me wait!"— but well I know
    She took a good half-hour to loose and lay
Those locks in dazzling disarrangement so!

A HYMN OF HOPE

FOR THE HUNDREDTH ANNIVERSARY OF PHILLIPS
EXETER ACADEMY

HAS, then, our boyhood vanished,
   And rosy morning fled?
Are faith and ardor banished,
   Is daring courage dead?
Still runs the olden river
   By meadow, hill, and wood, —
Where are the hearts that ever
   Beat high with royal blood?

The golden dreams we cherished
   Pacing the ancient town, —
Have they but bloomed and perished,
   And flown like thistledown?
Nay, still the air is haunted
   With mystery as of old;
Each blossom is enchanted,
   And every leaflet's fold.

Not one fair hope we hearkened,
   But still to youth returns;
Not one clear light hath darkened, —
   Still for some breast it burns:

Though age by age is lying
    Beneath the gathering mould,
Life's dawn-light is undying,
    Its dreams grow never old.

As the great faithful planet
    Goes plunging on its track,
Thought still shall bravely man it,
    And steer through storm and wrack;
While but three souls are toiling
    Who would give all for right,
Whom gold nor fame is spoiling,
    Whose prayer is but for light;

While there are found a handful
    Of spirits vowed to truth,
Clear-eyed, courageous, manful,
    And comrades as in youth;
Out of the darkness sunward,
    Out of the night to day,
While all the worlds swing onward,
    Life shall not lose its way.

When to the man-soul lonely
    The loving gods came down,
Earth gave the mantle only,
    Free mind the immortal crown.
Wild force with cloud-wraith stature
    Unsealed shall tower in vain,

And the fierce Afreet, Nature,
  Obey the sceptred brain.

O heart of man immortal,
  Beat on in love and cheer!
Somewhere the cloudy portal
  Of all thy prayers shall clear.
The fair earth's mighty measure
  Of life, untouched by rime,
Through star-dust and through azure
  Rolls on to endless time.

The power that motes inherit,
  That bud and crystal find,
Hath not forgotten spirit,
  Nor left the soul behind.
O'er Time's dumb forces fleeting
  This victory we begin,
Dear eye-beams and the beating
  Of heart with heart shall win.

AN ANCIENT ERROR

He that has and a little tiny wit, —
With hey, ho, the wind and the rain. — Lear

The " sobbing wind," the " weeping rain," —
   'T is time to give the lie
To these old superstitions twain,
   That poets sing and sigh.

Taste the sweet drops, — no tang of brine ;
   Feel them, — they do not burn ;
The daisy-buds, whereon they shine,
   Laugh, and to blossoms turn.

There is no natural grief or sin ;
   'T is we have flung the pall,
And brought the sound of sorrow in.
   Pan is not dead at all.

The merry Pan ! his blithesome look
   Twinkles through sun and rain ;
By ivied rock and rippled brook
   He pipes his jocund strain.

If winds have wailed and skies wept tears,
   To poet's vision dim,

'T was that his own sobs filled his ears,
  His weeping blinded him.

'T is laughing breeze and singing shower,
  As ever heart could need;
And who with " hey " and " ho " must lower
  Hath " tiny wit " indeed.

AN ADAGE FROM THE ORIENT

AT the punch-bowl's brink,
Let the thirsty think
What they say in Japan:

" First the man takes a drink,
Then the drink takes a drink,
Then the drink takes the man ! "

TO A MAID DEMURE

OFTEN when the night is come,
With its quiet group at home,
While they broider, knit, or sew,
Read, or chat in voices low,
Suddenly you lift your eyes
With an earnest look, and wise;
But I cannot read their lore, —
Tell me less, or tell me more.

Like a picture in a book,
Pure and peaceful is your look,
Quietly you walk your ways;
Steadfast duty fills the days.
Neither tears nor fierce delights,
Feverish days nor tossing nights,
Any troublous dreams confess, —
Tell me more, or tell me less.

Swift the weeks are on the wing;
Years are brief, and love a thing
Blooming, fading, like a flower;
Wake and seize the little hour.
Give me welcome, or farewell;
Quick! I wait! And who can tell
What to-morrow may befall, —
Love me more, or not at all.

HERMIONE

I

THE LOST MAGIC

WHITE in her snowy stone, and cold,
　　With azure veins and shining arms,
Pygmalion doth his bride behold,
　　Rapt on her pure and sculptured charms.

Ah! in those half-divine old days
　　Love still worked miracles for men;
The gods taught lovers wondrous ways
　　To breathe a soul in marble then.

He gazed, he yearned, he vowed, he wept.
　　Some secret witchery touched her breast;
And, laughing April tears, she stepped
　　Down to his arms and lay at rest.

Dear artist of the storied land!
　　I too have loved a heart of stone.
What was thy charm of voice or hand,
　　Thy secret spell, Pygmalion?

II

INFLUENCES

If quiet autumn mornings would not come,
With golden light, and haze, and harvest wain,
And spices of the dead leaves at my feet;
If sunsets would not burn through cloud, and stain
With fading rosy flush the dusky dome;
If the young mother would not croon that sweet
Old sleep-song, like the robin's in the rain;
If the great cloud-ships would not float and drift
Across such blue all the calm afternoon;
If night were not so hushed; or if the moon
Might pause forever by that pearly rift,
Nor fill the garden with its flood again;
If the world were not what it still must be,
Then might I live forgetting love and thee.

III

THE DEAD LETTER

The letter came at last. I carried it
To the deep woods unopened. All the trees
Were hushed, as if they waited what was writ,
And feared for me. Silent they let me sit
Among them; leaning breathless while I read,
And bending down above me where they stood.
A long way off I heard the delicate tread
Of the light-footed loiterer, the breeze,
Come walking toward me in the leafy wood.

I burned the page that brought me love and woe.
At first it writhed to feel the spires of flame,
Then lay quite still; and o'er each word there came
Its white ghost of the ash, and burning slow
Each said: "You cannot kill the spirit; know
That we shall haunt you, even till heart and brain
Lie as we lie in ashes — all in vain."

IV

THE SONG IN THE NIGHT

In the deep night a little bird
    Wakens, or dreams he is awake:
Cheerily clear one phrase is heard,
    And you almost feel the morning break.

In the deep dark of loss and wrong,
    One face like a lovely dawn will thrill,
And all night long at my heart a song
    Suddenly stirs and then is still.

TRUTH AT LAST

Does a man ever give up hope, I wonder, —
Face the grim fact, seeing it clear as day?
When Bennen saw the snow slip, heard its thunder
Low, louder, roaring round him, felt the speed
Grow swifter as the avalanche hurled downward,
Did he for just one heart-throb — did he indeed
Know with all certainty, as they swept onward,
There was the end, where the crag dropped away?
Or did he think, even till they plunged and fell,
Some miracle would stop them? Nay, they tell
That he turned round, face forward, calm and pale,
Stretching his arms out toward his native vale
As if in mute, unspeakable farewell,
And so went down. — 'T is something, if at last,
Though only for a flash, a man may see
Clear-eyed the future as he sees the past,
From doubt, or fear, or hope's illusion free.

UNTIMELY THOUGHT

I LOOKED across the lawn one summer's day,
  Deep shadowed, dreaming in the drowsy light,
  And thought, what if this afternoon, so bright
And still, should end it ? — as it may.

Blue dome, and flocks of fleece that slowly pass
  Before the pale old moon, the while she keeps
  Her sleepy watch, and ancient pear that sweeps
Its low, fruit-laden skirts along the grass.

What if I had to say to all of these,
  " So this is the last time " — suddenly there
My love came loitering under the great trees ;

  And now the thought I could no longer bear :
Startled I flung it from me, as one flings
All sharply from the hand a bee that stings.

SERVICE

FRET not that the day is gone,
And thy task is still undone.
'Twas not thine, it seems, at all:
Near to thee it chanced to fall,
Close enough to stir thy brain,
And to vex thy heart in vain.
Somewhere, in a nook forlorn,
Yesterday a babe was born:
He shall do thy waiting task;
All thy questions he shall ask,
And the answers will be given,
Whispered lightly out of heaven.
His shall be no stumbling feet,
Falling where they should be fleet:
He shall hold no broken clue;
Friends shall unto him be true;
Men shall love him; falsehood's aim
Shall not shatter his good name.
Day shall nerve his arm with light,
Slumber soothe him all the night;
Summer's peace and winter's storm
Help him all his will perform.
'T is enough of joy for thee
His high service to foresee.

ON A PICTURE OF MT. SHASTA BY KEITH

Two craggy slopes, sheer down on either hand,
Fall to a cleft, dark and confused with pines.
Out of their sombre shade — one gleam of light —
Escaping toward us like a hurrying child,
Half laughing, half afraid, a white brook runs.
The fancy tracks it back through the thick gloom
Of crowded trees, immense, mysterious
As monoliths of some colossal temple,
Dusky with incense, chill with endless time :
Through their dim arches chants the distant wind,
Hollow and vast, and ancient oracles
Whisper, and wait to be interpreted.
Far up the gorge denser and darker grows
The forest ; columns lie with writhen roots in air,
And across open glades the sunbeams slant
To touch the vanishing wing-tips of shy birds ;
Till from a mist-rolled valley soar the slopes,
Blue-hazy, dense with pines to the verge of snow,
Up into cloud. Suddenly parts the cloud,
And lo ! in heaven — as pure as very snow,
Uplifted like a solitary world —
A star, grown all at once distinct and clear, —
The white earth-spirit, Shasta ! Calm, alone,

THE WHITE EARTH-SPIRIT, SHASTA!

Silent it stands, cold in the crystal air,
White-bosomed sister of the stainless dawn,
With whom the cloud holds converse, and the storm
Rests there, and stills its tempest into snow.

Once — you remember ? — we beheld that vision,
But busy days recalled us, and the whole
Fades now among my memories like a dream.
The distant thing is all incredible,
And the dim past as if it had not been.
Our world flees from us; only the one point,
The unsubstantial moment, is our own.
We are but as the dead, save that swift mote
Of conscious life. Then the great artist comes,
Commands the chariot wheels of Time to stay,
Summons the distant, as by some austere
Grand gesture of a mighty sorcerer's wand,
And our whole world again becomes our own.
So we escape the petty tyranny
Of the incessant hour; pure thought evades
Its customary bondage, and the mind
Is lifted up, watching the moon-like globe.

How should a man be eager or perturbed
Within this calm ? How should he greatly care
For reparation, or redress of wrong, —
To scotch the liar, or spurn the fawning knave,
Or heed the babble of the ignoble crew ?
Seest thou yon blur far up the icy slope,

Like a man's footprint ? Half thy little town
Might hide there, or be buried in what seems
From yonder cliff a curl of feathery snow.
Still the far peak would keep its frozen calm,
Still at the evening on its pinnacle
Would the one tender touch of sunset dwell,
And o'er it nightlong wheel the silent stars.
So the great globe rounds on, — mountains, and vales,
Forests, waste stretches of gaunt rock and sand,
Shore, and the swaying ocean, — league on league ;
And blossoms open, and are sealed in frost ;
And babes are born, and men are laid to rest.
What is this breathing atom, that his brain
Should build or purpose aught or aught desire,
But stand a moment in amaze and awe,
Rapt on the wonderfulness of the world ?

"QUEM METUI MORITURA?"

ÆNEID, IV. 604

WHAT need have I to fear — so soon to die?
  Let me work on, not watch and wait in dread:
  What will it matter, when that I am dead,
That they bore hate or love who near me lie?
'T is but a lifetime, and the end is nigh
  At best or worst. Let me lift up my head
  And firmly, as with inner courage, tread
Mine own appointed way, on mandates high.
Pain could but bring, from all its evil store,
  The close of pain: hate's venom could but kill;
Repulse, defeat, desertion, could no more.
  Let me have lived my life, not cowered until
The unhindered and unhastened hour was here.
So soon — what is there in the world to fear?

THE SINGER

SILLY bird!
When his mate is near,
Not a note of singing shall you hear.
Take his little love away,
Half the livelong day
Will his tune be heard —
Silly bird!

Sunny days
Silent basks he in the light,
Little sybarite!
But when all the room
Darkens in the gloom,
And the rain
Pours and pours along the pane,
He is bent
(Ah, the small inconsequent!)
On defying all the weather;
Rain and cloud and storm together
Naught to him,
Singing like the seraphim.

So we know a poet's ways:
Sunny days,

Silent he
In his fine serenity;
But if winds are loud,
He will pipe beneath the cloud;
And if one is far away,
Sings his heart out, as to say, —
" It may be
She will hear and come to me."

WORDSWORTH

A MOONLIT desert's yellow sands,
Where, dimmer than its shadow, stands
A motionless palm-tree here and there,
And the great stars through amber air
Burn calm as planets, and the face
Of earth seems lifting into space : —

A tropic ocean's starlit rest,
Along whose smooth and sleeping breast
Slow swells just stir the mirrored gleams,
Like faintest sighs in placid dreams ;
All overhead the night, so high
And hollow that there seems no sky,
But the unfathomed deeps, among
The worlds down endless arches swung : —

On moonlit plain, and starlit sea,
Is life's lost charm, tranquillity.

A poet found it once, and took
It home, and hid it in a book,
As one might press a violet.
There still the odor lingers yet.
Delicious ; from your treasured tomes

Reach down your Wordsworth, and there comes
That fragrance which no bard but he
E'er caught, as if the plain and sea
Had yielded their serenity.

THE WORLD RUNS ROUND

For the Anniversary of the "Overland Magazine,"
San Francisco, 1884

The world runs round,
And the world runs well;
And at heaven's bound,
Weaving what the hours shall tell
Of the future way,
Sit the great Norns, sisters gray.
Now a thread of doom and hate,
Now a skein of life and love, —
Whether hearing shriek or psalm,
Hearts that curse or pray,
Most composed and very calm
Is their weaving, soon and late.

One man's noisy years go by,
Rich to the crowd's shallow eye,
Full of big and empty sound,
Brandished gesture, voice profound,
Blustering benevolence,
Thin in deeds and poor in pence.
Out of it all, so loud and long,
What one thread that's clean and strong
To weave the coming good,
Can the great Norns find?

But where some poor child stood,
And shrank, and wept its faultiness,
Out of that little life so blind
The great web takes a golden strand
That shall shine and that shall stand
The whole wide world to bless.

One man walks in silk:
Honey and milk
Flow through his days.
Corn loads his wains,
He hath all men's praise,
He sees his heart's desire.
In all his veins
What can the sorrowful Norns
Find of heroic fire?
Another finds his ways
All blocked and barred
Lonely, he grapples hard,
Sets teeth and bleeds.
Then the glad Norns
Know he succeeds,
With victory wrought
Greater than he sought.

When will the world believe
Force is for him that is met and fought:
Storm hath no song till the pine resists;
Lightning no flame when it runs as it lists;

So do the wise Norns weave.
The world runs round,
And the world runs well:
It needs no prophet, when evil is found,
Good to foretell.

Many the voices
Ruffling the air:
This one rejoices,
That in despair
Past the sky-bars
Climbs to the stars.

One voice is heard
By the ocean's shore,
Speaking a word
Quiet and sane,
Amid the human rush and roar
Like a robin's song in the rain.
The red gold of the sun
Seems to stream in power
Already from behind the shower
When that song's begun.

It doth not insist, or claim;
You may hear, or go:
It clamors not for gain or fame,
Tranquilly and slow
It speaketh unafraid,

Calls the spade, spade,
With the large sense mature
Of him that hath both sat and roved,
And with a solemn undercurrent pure,
As his that now hath lived and loved.
Brightened with glimpse and gleam
Of mother-wit —
There is more salt in it,
More germ and sperm
Of the great things to be,
Than louder notes men speak and sing.

It is a voice of Spring,
Clear and firm.
Tones prophetic in it flow,
Steady and strong,
Yet soft and low —
An excellent thing in song.
" I can wait," saith merry Spring ;
If the rain runneth, and the wind hummeth,
And the mount at morn be hoar with snow,
In the frost the violet dozes,
Wind and rain bear breath of roses,
And the great summer cometh
Wherein all things shall gayly bloom and grow.
Long may the voice be found,
Potent its spell,
While the world runs round,
And the world runs well.

CARPE DIEM

How the dull thought smites me dumb,
" It will come ! " and " It will come ! "
But to-day I am not dead ;
Life in hand and foot and head
Leads me on its wondrous ways.
'T is in such poor, common days,
Made of morning, noon, and night,
Golden truth has leaped to light,
Potent messages have sped,
Torches flashed with running rays,
World-runes started on their flight.

Let it come, when come it must ;
But To-Day from out the dust
Blooms and brightens like a flower,
Fair with love, and faith, and power.
Pluck it with unclouded will,
From the great tree Igdrasil.

By courtesy of the Soule Art Publishing Co.

AMONG THE REDWOODS

AMONG THE REDWOODS

Farewell to such a world! Too long I press
 The crowded pavement with unwilling feet.
Pity makes pride, and hate breeds hatefulness,
 And both are poisons. In the forest, sweet
The shade, the peace! Immensity, that seems
To drown the human life of doubts and dreams.

Far off the massive portals of the wood,
 Buttressed with shadow, misty-blue, serene,
Waited my coming. Speedily I stood
 Where the dun wall rose roofed in plumy green.
Dare one go in? — Glance backward! Dusk as
  night
Each column, fringed with sprays of amber light.

Let me, along this fallen bole, at rest,
 Turn to the cool, dim roof my glowing face.
Delicious dark on weary eyelids prest!
 Enormous solitude of silent space,
But for a low and thunderous ocean sound,
Too far to hear, felt thrilling through the ground!

No stir nor call the sacred hush profanes;
 Save when from some bare treetop, far on high,

Fierce disputations of the clamorous cranes
    Fall muffled, as from out the upper sky.
So still, one dreads to wake the dreaming air,
Breaks a twig softly, moves the foot with care.

The hollow dome is green with empty shade,
    Struck through with slanted shafts of afternoon;
Aloft, a little rift of blue is made,
    Where slips a ghost that last night was the moon;
Beside its pearl a sea-cloud stays its wing,
Beneath a tilted hawk is balancing.

The heart feels not in every time and mood
    What is around it. Dull as any stone
I lay; then, like a darkening dream, the wood
    Grew Karnak's temple, where I breathed alone
In the awed air strange incense, and uprose
Dim, monstrous columns in their dread repose.

The mind not always sees; but if there shine
    A bit of fern-lace bending over moss,
A silky glint that rides a spider-line,
    On a trefoil two shadow-spears that cross,
Three grasses that toss up their nodding heads,
With spring and curve like clustered fountain
        threads, —

Suddenly, through side windows of the eye,
    Deep solitudes, where never souls have met;

Vast spaces, forest corridors that lie
   In a mysterious world, unpeopled yet.
Because the outward eye elsewhere was caught,
The awfulness and wonder come unsought.

If death be but resolving back again
   Into the world's deep soul, this is a kind
Of quiet, happy death, untouched by pain
   Or sharp reluctance. For I feel my mind
Is interfused with all I hear and see;
As much a part of All as cloud or tree.

Listen! A deep and solemn wind on high;
   The shafts of shining dust shift to and fro;
The columned trees sway imperceptibly,
   And creak as mighty masts when trade-winds blow.
The cloudy sails are set; the earth-ship swings
Along the sea of space to grander things.

AT DAWN

I LAY awake and listened, ere the light
Began to whiten at the window pane.
The world was all asleep: earth was a fane
Emptied of worshipers; its dome of night,
Its silent aisles, were awful in their gloom.
Suddenly from the tower the bell struck four,
Solemn and slow, how slow and solemn! o'er
Those death-like slumberers, each within his room.
The last reverberation pulsed so long
It seemed no tone of earthly mould at all.
But the bell woke a thrush; and with a call
He roused his mate, then poured a tide of song:
" Morning is coming, fresh, and clear, and blue,"
Said that bright song; and then I thought of you.

HER FACE

I STOOD in sombre dreaming
  Before her image dear,
And saw, in secret wonder,
  Living my darling appear.

About her mouth a smile came,
  So wonderful and wise,
And tears of some still sorrow
  Seemed shining in her eyes.

My tears, they too were flowing,
  Her face I could not see,
And oh! I cannot believe it,
  That my love is lost to me.

LATER POEMS

A MORNING THOUGHT

What if some morning, when the stars were paling,
    And the dawn whitened, and the East was clear,
Strange peace and rest fell on me from the presence
    Of a benignant Spirit standing near:

And I should tell him, as he stood beside me,
    "This is our Earth — most friendly Earth, and
        fair;
Daily its sea and shore through sun and shadow
    Faithful it turns, robed in its azure air:

"There is blest living here, loving and serving,
    And quest of truth, and serene friendships dear;
But stay not, Spirit! Earth has one destroyer, —
    His name is Death: flee, lest he find thee here!"

And what if then, while the still morning brightened,
    And freshened in the elm the Summer's breath,
Should gravely smile on me the gentle angel
    And take my hand and say, "My name is Death!"

STRANGE

HE died at night. Next day they came
To weep and praise him : sudden fame
These suddenly warm comrades gave.
They called him pure, they called him brave;
One praised his heart, and one his brain;
All said, You'd seek his like in vain, —
Gentle, and strong, and good: none saw
In all his character a flaw.

At noon he wakened from his trance,
Mended, was well! They looked askance;
Took his hand coldly; loved him not,
Though they had wept him; quite forgot
His virtues; lent an easy ear
To slanderous tongues; professed a fear
He was not what he seemed to be;
Thanked God they were not such as he;
Gave to his hunger stones for bread;
And made him, living, wish him dead.

MOODS

Dawn has blossomed: the sun is nigh:
Pearl and rose in the wimpled sky,
Rose and pearl on a brightening blue.
(She is true, and she is true!)

The noonday lies all warm and still
And calm, and over sleeping hill
And wheatfields falls a dreamy hue.
(If she be true — if she be true!)

The patient evening comes, most sad and fair:
Veiled are the stars; the dim and quiet air
Breathes bitter scents of hidden myrrh and rue.
(If she were true — if she were only true!)

THE BOOK OF HOURS

As one who reads a tale writ in a tongue
   He only partly knows, — runs over it
   And follows but the story, losing wit
And charm, and half the subtle links among
The haps and harms that the book's folk beset, —
   So do we with our life. Night comes, and morn:
   I know that one has died and one is born;
That this by love and that by hate is met.
But all the grace and glory of it fail
   To touch me, and the meanings they enfold.
The Spirit of the World hath told the tale,
   And tells it: and 't is very wise and old.
But o'er the page there is a mist and veil:
   I do not know the tongue in which 't is told.

"WORDS, WORDS, WORDS"

TO ONE WHO FLOUTED THEM AS VAIN

I

Am I not weary of them as your heart
Or ever Hamlet's was? — the empty ones,
Mere breath of passing air, mere hollow tones
That idle winds to broken reeds impart.

Have they not cursed my life? — sounds I mistook
For sacred verities, — love, faith, delight,
And the sweet tales that women tell at night,
When darkness hides the falsehood of the look.

I was the one of all Ulysses' crew
(What time he stopped their ears) that leaped and fled
Unto the sirens, for the honey-dew

Of their dear songs. The poets me have fed
With the same poisoned fruit. And even you, —
Did you not pluck them for me in days dead?

II

Nay, they do bear a blessing and a power, —
Great words and true, that bridge from soul to soul
The awful cloud-depths that betwixt us roll.
I will not have them so blasphemed. This hour,

This little hour of life, this lean to-day, —
What were it worth but for those mighty dreams
That sweep from down the past on sounding streams
Of such high-thoughted words as poets say ?

What, but for Shakespeare's and for Homer's lay,
And bards whose sacred names all lips repeat ?
Words, — only words ; yet, save for tongue and pen

Of those great givers of them unto men,
And burdens they still bear of grave or sweet,
This world were but for beasts, a darkling den.

FOUR SONNETS FROM SULLY PRUD-HOMME

SIESTA

ALL summer let me lie along the grass,
   Hands under head, and lids that almost close;
   Nor mix a sigh with breathings of the rose,
Nor vex light-sleeping echo with "Alas!"
Fearless, I will abandon blood, and limb,
   And very soul to the all-changing hours;
   In calmness letting the unnumbered powers
Of nature weave my rest into their hymn.
Beneath the sunshine's golden tent uplift
   Mine eyes shall watch the upper blue unfurled,
Till its deep joy into my heart shall sift
   Through lashes linked, and, dreaming on the world,
Its love and hate, or memories far of these,
Shall lull me like the sound of distant seas.

THE CLOUD

Couched on the turf, and lying mute and still,
  While the deep heaven lifts higher and more pure,
  I love to watch, as if some hidden lure
It followed, one light cloud above the hill.
The flitting film takes many an aspect strange:
  An orchard's snow; a far-off, sunlit sail;
  A fleck of foam; a seraph's floating veil.
We see it altered, never see it change.
Now a soft shred detaches, fades from sight;
  Another comes, melts, and the blue is clear
And clearer, as when breath has dimmed the steel.
  Such is my changeful spirit, year by year:
A sigh, the soul of such a cloud, as light
And vanishing, lost in the infinite.

IN SEPARATION

The bliss that happy lovers dream will bloom
  Forever new shall scarce outlast the year:
  Their calmer kisses wake nor smile nor tear;
Love's nesting-place already is its tomb,
Since sated eyes grow weary of their prey,
And constant vows their own best hopes betray,
And love's June lily, marred but by a breath,
Falls where the other lilies lie in death,
Therefore the doom of land and sea that bar
  My life from hers I do accept. At least
  No passion will rise jaded from the feast,

My pure respect no passing fires can stain;
So without hope I love her, without pain,
Without desire, as one might love a star.

L'AMOUR ASSASSINÉ

Poor wretch! that smites, in his despair insane,
　The tender mouth for which he has no bread,
　And in some lonely spot, ere it be dead,
Covers the little corse, yet warm, ill-slain :
So I struck down dear Love for being born!
　I smoothed the limbs, and closed the eyes, and lone
　The darling form was left, 'neath ponderous stones;
Then, at my deed dismayed, I fled forlorn.
I deemed my love was dead indeed, in vain!
　Erect he speaks, close by the open tomb,
　'Mid April lilacs even there in bloom,
　With immortelles his pale brow glorified :
"Thou didst but wound ; I live to seek her side ;
Not by thy hand, not thine, can I be slain!"

MY PEACE THOU ART

AFTER SCHUBERT'S " DU BIST MEIN' RUH' "

My peace thou art, thou art my rest ;
From thee my pain, in thee so blest :
Enter mine eyes, this heart draw near ;
Oh come, oh dwell forever here.

Enter, and close the door, and come,
And be this breast thine endless home ;
Shut out all lesser care and woe,
I would thy hurt and healing know.

Clear light that on my soul hath shone,
Still let it shine from thee alone,
                    From thee alone.

MIR AUS DEN AUGEN

FROM A POLISH SONG OF CHOPIN

" Away ! Let not mine eyes, my heart, behold you ! "
   It was your right to choose ; I heard you say,
" Forget ! We must forget ! " Love might have told
     you
   'T was vain. You could not, more than I, obey.

As the dim shadows down the pastures lengthen,
   The further sinks the day-star's fading fire,
So in your breast will tender memories strengthen,
   Deeper and darker as my steps retire.

At every hour, in every place of meeting,
   Where we together shared delight and pain,
Yes, everywhere will dear thoughts keep repeating,
   "Here, too, his voice, his look, his touch, remain ! "

THE ORACLE

Down in its crystal hollow
  Gleams the ebon well of ink:
In the deepest drop lies lurking
  The thought all men shall think.

Fair on the waiting tablet
  Lies the empty paper's space:
Out of its snow shall flush a word
  Like an angel's earnest face.

Who in those depths shall cast his line
  For the gnome that hugs that thought?
Who from the snowy field shall charm
  That flower of truth untaught?

Not in the lore of the ancients,
  Not in the yesterday:
On the lips of the living moments
  The gods their message lay.

Somewhere near it is waiting,
  Like a night-wind wandering free,
Seeking a mouth to speak through, —
  Whose shall the message be?

It may steal forth like a flute note,
   It may be suddenly hurled
In blare upon blare of a trumpet blast,
   To startle and stir the world.

Hark! but just on the other side
   Some thinnest wall of dreams,
Murmurs a whispered music,
   And softest rose-light gleams.

Listen, and watch, and tell the world
   What it almost dies to know:
Or wait — and the wise old world will say,
   " I knew it long ago."

TEMPTED

Yes, I know what you say :
  Since it cannot be soul to soul,
Be it flesh to flesh, as it may ;
  But is Earth the whole ?

Shall a man betray the Past
  For all Earth gives ?
" But the Past is dead ? " At last,
  It is all that lives.

Which were the nobler goal —
  To snatch at the moment's bliss,
Or to swear I will keep my soul
  Clean for her kiss ?

FORCE

THE stars know a secret
  They do not tell;
And morn brings a message
  Hidden well.

There's a blush on the apple,
  A tint on the wing,
And the bright wind whistles,
  And the pulses sting.

Perish dark memories!
  There's light ahead;
This world's for the living;
  Not for the dead.

In the shining city,
  On the loud pave,
The life-tide is running
  Like a leaping wave.

How the stream quickens,
  As noon draws near,
No room for loiterers,
  No time for fear.

Out on the farm lands
   Earth smiles as well;
Gold-crusted grain-fields,
   With sweet, warm smell;

Whir of the reaper,
   Like a giant bee;
Like a Titan cricket,
   Thrilling with glee.

On mart and meadow,
   Pavement or plain,
On azure mountain,
   Or azure main —

Heaven bends in blessing;
   Lost is but won;
Goes the good rain-cloud,
   Comes the good sun!

Only babes whimper,
   And sick men wail,
And faint hearts and feeble hearts
   And weaklings fail.

Down the great currents
   Let the boat swing;
There was never winter
   But brought the spring.

INFIRMITY

WHAT is the truth to believe,
   What is the right to be done?
Caught in the webs I weave
   I halt from sun to sun.

The bright wind flows along,
   Calm nature's streaming law,
And its stroke is soft and strong
   As a leopard's velvet paw.

Free of the doubting mind,
   Full of the olden power,
Are the tree, and the bee, and the wind,
   And the wren, and the brave may-flower.

Man was the last to appear,
   A glow at the close of day;
Slow clambering now in fear
   He gropes his slackened way.

All the up-thrust is gone,
   Force that came from of old,
Up through the fish, and the swan,
   And the sea-king's mighty mould.

The youth of the world is fled,
   There are omens in the sky,
Spheres that are chilled and dead,
   And the close of an age is nigh.

The time is too short to grieve,
   Or to choose, for the end is one:
And what is the truth to believe,
   And what is the right to be done?

HER EXPLANATION

So you have wondered at me, — guessed in vain
What the real woman is you know so well?
    I am a lost illusion. Some strange spell
Once made your friend there, with his fine disdain
Of fact, conceive me perfect. He would fain
    (But could not) see me always, as befell
    His dream to see me, plucking asphodel,
In saffron robes, on some celestial plain.
All that I was he marred and flung away
    In quest of what I was not, could not be, —
    Lilith, or Helen, or Antigone.
Still he may search; but I have had my day,
    And now the Past is all the part for me
That this world's empty stage has left to play.

WARNING

BE true to me! For there will dawn a day
When thou wilt find the faith that now I see,
Bow at the shrines where I must bend the knee,
Knowing the great from small. Then lest thou say,
"Ah me, that I had never flung away
His love who would have stood so close to me
Where now I walk alone,"— lest there should be
Such vain regret, Love, oh, be true! But nay,
Not true to me: true to thine own high quest
Of truth; the aspiration in thy breast,
Noble and blind, that pushes by my hand,
And will not lean, yet cannot surely stand;
True to thine own pure heart, as mine to thee
Beats true. So shalt thou best be true to me.

AT EARLY MORN

WALK who will at deep of noon,
Or stroll fantastic in the moon;
I would take the morning earth,
New as at creation's birth,
Air unbreathed, and grass untrod;
Where I cross the dawn-lit sod,
Making green paths in the gray
Of the dew that's brushed away.

Would some depth of holy night,
Sacred with its starry light,
Over all my breast might roll,
Bringing dawn unto my soul,
That its consecrated dew
Might refresh and make me new!
Then that thou and I might pace
Some far planet, poised in space,
Fresh as children innocent,
In each other's love content!
There our feet should recommence,
Lightened of experience,
Morning ways on dewy slope,
Winged with wonder and with hope;
All the things we'd thought, or done,
Or felt before, forgot — save one!

SUMMER NIGHT

FROM the warm garden in the summer night
All faintest odors came: the tuberose white
Glimmered in its dark bed, and many a bloom
Invisibly breathed spices on the gloom.
It stirred a trouble in the man's dull heart,
A vexing, mute unrest: "Now what thou art,
Tell me!" he said in anger. Something sighed,
"I am the poor ghost of a ghost that died
In years gone by." And he recalled of old
A passion dead — long dead, even then — that came
And haunted many a night like this, the same
In their dim hush above the fragrant mould
And glimmering flowers, and troubled all his breast.
"Rest!" then he cried; "perturbèd spirit, rest!"

HIS NEIGHBOR AS HIMSELF

BLACK the storming ocean, crests that leap and
        whelm;
Ship a tumbling ruin, stripped of spar and helm.
Now she shudders upward, strangled with a sea;
Then she hangs a moment, and the moon breaks free
On her huddled creatures, waiting but to drown,
As she reels and staggers, ready to go down.

Crash! the glassy mountain whirls her to her grave.
In the foam three struggle; one his love will save.
There's a plank for two, but, as he lifts her there,
Lo! his rival sinking; eyes that clutch despair.
Only a swift instant left him to decide, —
Shall he drown, and yield the other life and bride?

In the peaceful morning stays a snowy sail.
Two afloat, — one missing. Which one? Did he
        fail, —
Coward, merely man? Or did the great sea darken
        eyes
All divinely shining with self-sacrifice?

NIGHT AND PEACE

NIGHT in the woods, — night :
  Peace, peace on the plain.
The last red sunset beam
  Belts the tall beech with gold ;
  The quiet kine are in the fold,
And stilly flows the stream.
  Soon shall we see the stars again,
  For one more day down to its rest has lain,
And all its cares have taken flight,
  And all its doubt and pain.
Night in the woods, — night :
  Peace, peace on the plain.

THE PHILOSOPHER

His wheel of logic whirled and spun all day;
All day he held his system, grinding it
Finer and finer, till 't was fined away.

But the chance sparks of sense and mother-wit,
Flung out as that wheel-logic spun and whirled,
Kindled the nations, and lit up the world.

HIS LOST DAY

Growing old, and looking back
Wistfully along his track,
I have heard him try to tell,
With a smile a little grim,
Why a world he loved so well
Had no larger fruit of him : —

'T was one summer, when the time
Loiterèd like drowsy rhyme,
Sauntering on his idle way
Somehow he had lost a day.
Whether 't was the daisies meek,
Keeping Sabbath all the week,
Birds without one work-day even,
Or the little pagan bees,
Busy all the sunny seven, —
Whether sleep at afternoon,
Or much rising with the moon,
Couching with the morning star,
Or enchantments like to these,
Had confused his calendar, —
"It is Saturday," men said.
"Nay, 't is Friday," obstinate
Clung the notion in his head.

Had the cloudy sisters three,
In their weaving of his fate,
Dozed, and dropped a stitch astray ?

" 'T was the losing of that day
  Cost my fortune," he would say.
" On that day I should have writ
  Screeds of wisdom and of wit;
  Should have sung the missing song,
  Wonderful, and sweet, and strong ;
  Might have solved men's doubt and dream
  With some waiting truth supreme.
  If another thing there be
  That a groping hand may miss
  In a twilight world like this,
  Those lost hours its grace and glee
  Surely would have brought to me."

FULFILLMENT

ALL the skies had gloomed in gray,
Many a week, day after day.
Nothing came the blank to fill,
Nothing stirred the stagnant will.
Winds were raw; buds would not swell:
Some malign and sullen spell
Soured the currents of the year,
And filled the heart with lurking fear.

In his room he moped and glowered,
Where the leaden daylight lowered;
Drummed the casement, turned his book,
Hating nature's hostile look.

Suddenly there came a day
When he flung his gloom away.
Something hinted help was near:
Winds were fresh and sky was clear;
Light he stepped, and firmly planned, —
Some good news was close at hand

Truly: for when day was done,
He was lying all alone,

Fretted pulse had ceased to beat,
Very still were hands and feet,
And the robins through the long
Twilight sang his slumber song.

THE RETURN TO ARCADIA

From Athens, Rome, and Asia,
The scattered troop returns. They are
Old comrades, who have felt, afar,
" *Et ego in Arcadia.*"

" Come, friends ! now that the table's cleared,
And flesh and fowl have disappeared,
Let us recount to one another
Our treatment from the world, our mother.
Urbanus, thou who hast a home
In the great metropole of Rome,
What canst thou say in blame or praise
Of the rich city's latest ways ? "

" What ! tempt an old boy thus to tell
Tales out of school ? Must I ? Ah, well,
Among ourselves perhaps I may :
For Rome it is the crisis-day.
The brave old city turns at bay
Against a vile barbarian crew;
Itself not pure as once : the new
Aristocrats, who've lately sprung
Like flaunting weeds from heaps of dung,
The *novi homines* — a breed

Of clowns that scarce their names can read,
Throng pave and palace, to display
The vulgar antics of the day.
Their wives, too senseless to be blamed,
Half naked and all unashamed,
Their sons with manners of the slave,
Their girls with morals of the pave,
These shine — a scum upon the stream
Of the great city of your dream.
The rich on harlots waste their store,
And brutish Gallic plays. The poor
Rot in their vermin, gnash their teeth,
And curse the feet they cower beneath.
Meantime the city fathers steal
The purses of the common weal.
But there are portents in the air :
The stern old Roman stuff is there,
Silent and grim. The other day,
A robber, swaggering with his prey
Past great *Justitia's* column, saw
Flash white the letters of the law,
And swift the statue's sleeping glaive
Fell ringing down and smote the knave ! "

" Now, *Atticus*, we fain would know
With thee and Athens how things go.
What of Brain-city ? Surely there
They breathe a somewhat purer air ? "

" Cold, cold, i' faith, and all too thin.
Their thinkers have abolished sin,
And virtue has become good taste.
They 've goodness, but it goes tight-laced.
Your true Athenian likes things new;
In all things superstitious, too.
No temples thronged like theirs ; at least
By women, amorous of the priest.
At knocking spirits they turn pale,
And trust the augurs' spectral tale ;
The sly old augurs ! who must wink
And nudge each other, when they think.
I saw a houseful on their knees
Before the ghost of Pericles —
Some lank Thessalian from the fleet,
Chalk-visaged, stalking in a sheet.
I saw a shrewd Ionian
Take forty *drachmae* from a man
For stroking his rheumatic limb,
And calling on the gods for him.
At every gleam of truth they blink,
Save what they think their neighbors think.
I hold with old Lucretius
Against their ghostly fudge and fuss.
When all their gods they glibly name,
And when I see this life of flame
That leaps in impotent despair
And breaks its heart upon the air,

I turn, O friends, with clasp of hands
For you — for the divine that stands
And faces me with human eyes
And living deeds and dear replies."

" Now, *Rusticus*, what of thy quest
Beyond the barriers of the West ? "

" The earth all right ; the world all wrong.
The birds are wise, the beasts are strong ;
The trees are virtuous, pure the air,
And field and farm and fold are fair ;
But as to men — ye know what are
The thick clods of Bœotia :
Too dull to read, too dull to think,
Brain-sodden, with the Celtic drink,
Till any demagogue may win
Their plaudits, plumed however thin.
In feverish towns impatient strive
The angry toilers of the hive,
Storing not honey, soon or late,
But venom of distrust and hate.
Bitter of heart, and blind of brain,
They grope for better things in vain,
And crouch like whipped hounds to the knaves
That boast them free to bind them slaves."

" And now, *Mugwumpius*, bard and seer,
How wags *thy* world, this many a year ?

Far hidden in thy mountain tower,
What is thy message of the hour ? "

" Like hurrying life, my thought I tell
In two words — welcome ! and farewell !
I 've trimmed my vines, and browned my hay,
And fed my pheasants of Cathay,
Watching you others try your wings,
And pondering on the world of things.
I trust the seasons, as they roll ;
I trust the striving human soul.
These ills and wrongs that gall and goad,
I count them all as episode ;
And far beyond these years I see
The dawn of golden destiny.
Welcome, oh, welcome ! — Nay, a bell
More solemn peals — farewell ! farewell ! "

THE BLOTTED PAGE

The Angel with the Book
    That holds each word and deed,
On my page let me look;
    And as I blushed to read, —

" Three things," the Angel said,
    " I may blot out for thee."
I bowed in thought my head —
    Now which ones should they be?

" Blot this!" — " No, that!" came quick,
    As still new conscience woke;
Till all the leaf was thick
    With blackening blur and stroke.

" 'T were better as I live,"
    I cried in my despair,
" To blot the whole, and give
    A new page otherwhere!"

LIVING

" To-day," I thought, " I will not plan nor strive ;
   Idle as yon blue sky, or clouds that go
   Like loitering ships, with sails as white as snow,
I simply will be glad to be alive."
   For, year by year, in steady summer glow
The flowers had bloomed, and life had stored its hive,
But tasted not the honey. Quite to thrive,
   The flavor of my thrift I now would know.
But the good breeze blew in a friend — a boon
   At any hour. There was a book to show,
     A gift to take, a slender one to give.
The morning passed to mellow afternoon,
And that to twilight ; it was sleep-time soon, —
     And lo ! again I had forgot to live.

BLINDFOLD

WHAT do we know of the world, as we grow so old
    and wise ?
Do the years, that still the heart-beats, quicken the
    drowsy eyes ?
At twenty we thought we knew it, — the world there,
    at our feet ;
We thought we had found its bitter, we knew we had
    found its sweet.
Now at forty and fifty, what do we make of the
    world ?
There in her sand she crouches, the Sphinx with her
    gray wings furled.
Soul of a man I know not ; who knoweth, can fore-
    tell,
And what can I read of fate, even of self I have
    learned so well ?
Heart of a woman I know not : how should I hope to
    know,
I that am foiled by a flower, or the stars of the silent
    snow ;
I that have never guessed the mind of the bright-eyed
    bird,
Whom even the dull rocks cheat, and the whirlwind's
    awful word ?

Let me loosen the fillet of clay from the shut and
    darkened lid,

For life is a blindfold game, and the Voice from view
    is hid.

I face him as best I can, still groping, here and there,

For the hand that has touched me lightly, the lips that
    have said, " Declare ! "

Well, I declare him my friend, — the friend of the
    whole sad race ;

And oh, that the game were over, and I might see his
    face !

But 't is much, though I grope in blindness, the Voice
    that is hid from view

May be heard, may be even loved, in a dream that
    may come true.

WIEGENLIED

Be still and sleep, my soul!
  Now gentle-footed Night,
In softly shadowed stole,
  Holds all the day from sight.

Why shouldst thou lie and stare
  Against the dark, and toss,
And live again thy care,
  Thine agony and loss?

'T was given thee to live,
  And thou hast lived it all;
Let that suffice, nor give
  One thought what may befall.

Thou hast no need to wake,
  Thou art no sentinel;
Love all the care will take,
  And Wisdom watcheth well.

Weep not, think not, but rest!
  The stars in silence roll;
On the world's mother-breast,
  Be still and sleep, my soul!

SIBYLLINE BARTERING

FATE, the gray Sibyl, with kind eyes above
  Closely locked lips, brought youth a merry crew
Of proffered friends; the price, self-slaying love.
  Proud youth repulsed them. She and they with-
    drew.

Then she brought half the troop; the cost, the same.
  My man's heart wavered : should I take the few,
And pay the whole ? But while I went and came,
  Fate had decided. She and they withdrew.

Once more she came, with two. Now life's midday
  Left fewer hours before me. Lonelier grew
The house and heart. But should the late purse pay
  The earlier price ? And she and they withdrew.

At last I saw Age his forerunners send.
  Then came the Sibyl, still with kindly eyes
And close-locked lips, and offered me one friend, —
  Thee, my one darling ! With what tears and cries

I claimed and claim thee ; ready now to pay
The perfect love that leaves no self to slay !

THE AGILE SONNETEER

How facile 't is to frame the sonnet! See:
  An "apt alliteration " at the start;
  Phrase fanciful, turned t'other-end-to with art;
And then a rhyme makes first and fourth agree.
Ee words enough — so this next quatrain we
  Will therefore rhyme to match. Here sometimes
    " heart "
  Comes in, as " hot " or " throbbing " to impart
A tang of sentiment to our idee.
Then the sextette, wherein there strictly ought
  To be a kind of winding up of things;
Only two rhymes (to have it nicely wrought)
  On which it settles, lark-like, as it sings.
  And so 't is perfect, head and tail and wings.
" Lacks something ? " Oh, as usual, but a thought.

MOMENTOUS WORDS

WHAT spiteful chance steals unawares
    Wherever lovers come,
And trips the nimblest brain and scares
    The bravest feelings dumb?

We had one minute at the gate,
    Before the others came;
To-morrow it would be too late,
    And whose would be the blame!

I gazed at her, she glanced at me;
    Alas! the time sped by:
"How warm it is to-day!" said she;
    "It looks like rain," said I.

THE CRICKETS IN THE FIELDS

One, or a thousand voices? — filling noon
   With such an undersong and drowsy chant
As sings in ears that waken from a swoon,
     And know not yet which world such murmurs
       haunt:
   Single, then double beats, reiterant;
Far off and near; one ceaseless, changeless tune.
If bird or breeze awake the dreamy will,
   We lose the song, as it had never been;
Then suddenly we find 't is singing still
     And had not ceased. — So, friend of mine, within
   My thoughts one underthought, beneath the din
Of life, doth every quiet moment fill.
Thy voice is far, thy face is hid from me,
But day and night are full of dreams of thee.

ALONE

STILL earth turns and pulses stir,
   And each day hath its deed;
But if I be dead to her,
   What is the life I lead?

Cares the cuckoo for the wood,
   When the red leaves are down?
Stays the robin near the brood,
   When they are fledged and flown?

Yea, we live; the common air
   To both its bounty brings.
Mockery! Can the absent share
   The half-forgotten things?

Barren comfort fancy doles
   To him that truly sees;
Sullen Earth can sever souls
   Far as the Pleiades.

Take thy toys, stepmother Earth, —
   Take force of limb and brain;
All thy gifts are little worth,
   Till her I find again.

Grass may spring and buds may stir,
    Why should mine eyes take heed?
For if I be dead to her,
    Then am I dead indeed.

BEFORE SUNRISE IN WINTER

A PURPLE cloud hangs half-way down;
    Sky, yellow gold below;
The naked trees, beyond the town,
    Like masts against it show —

Bare masts and spars of our earth-ship,
    With shining snow-sails furled;
And through the sea of space we slip,
    That flows all round the world.

ILLUSION

DAINTY Buttercup, my bird,
Dances at the mirror, stirred
By an ecstasy of song;
Tosses wing, pipes loud and long;
For this new mate, breast to breast,
Seems of golden birds the best.

Ah, my foolish little love,
Just such fantasy doth move
Your sweet spirit, when you find
Treasure in my heart or mind;
'T is not anything in me —
'T is your image that you see!

THE POET'S POLITICAL ECONOMY

THE round earth bears him without pay,
  Heaven brings sweet air to breathe,
Unto his brain each dying day
  Soft slumber doth bequeathe ;
Clear water runs in the mountain stream,
And sun gives glow, and star gives gleam.

O tiller of the wheat-land, give —
O miller by the brook-strand, give —
O shepherd, of thy fleeces give
The little that he needs to live.

He will never do ye wrong,
But pay in ringing gold of song.

A SUBTLETY

THEY were lovers when they wed.
　　Now some slight he showed to her
For another.　Then she said,
　　" Has it come that you prefer

Other women's good to mine ? "
　　" You and I are one," quoth he ;
" 'T is self-sacrifice, in fine,
　　To deny my other Me."

Silently she turns away,
　　Hiding tears that almost come.
In her heart I hear her say,
　　" Charity begins at home."

THE DIFFERENCE

In the morning the flowers blossomed
  All about my feet :
I did not stop to pick them,
  I scarcely knew them sweet.

Now in the dusky twilight
  Seeking with wistful care,
Not many I discover,
  And very few are fair.

A SONG IN THE AFTERNOON

COME, and let 's grow old,
  And let 's grow old together !
Boyhood's heart was wondrous bold,
  And light as any feather,
Rollicking and frolicking
  In every wind and weather ;
But come now, let 's grow old,
  And let 's grow old together !

Come and let 's be leal
  And true to one another !
Boys are fickle ; as they feel,
  So they do ; love this and t'other ;
Borrowing or sorrowing
  With any man and brother ;
But come now, let 's be leal
  And true to one another !

Come, and let 's be wise,
  And wag our heads sedately !
Cooler breezes clear the skies,
  And sight is lengthened greatly.
Jolly days were folly days ;
  We doff the motley lately.

So come now, let's be wise,
    And wag our heads sedately!

Come then, and let's grow old,
    So we grow old together!
Wits are thin o'er apple chin,
    Long beards give length of tether.
Spring may yearn, and summer burn,
    Your fall's the finest weather.
So come now, let's grow old,
    And let's grow old together!

A SUPPLICATION

MOTHER, O fair earth-mother!
Let not the hand of any other
Than thine own self, most wise and mild
Take the life of thy child.
Let not mine own folly,
Or murderous melancholy
Senseless and wild,
Or the blow of a madman's arm,
Do me that final harm.
Let rather one of thy great cliffs that fall
Bury me underneath its wall;
Or thine enormous sea
Sweep over me.
Whenever and however comes that day,
Take thou my life away.
So shall I seem to be a part
Of all thou art;
Mated with every noble natural form
Of thine eternal power;
A brother of the storm,
One kindred with the mountain and the flower.

SPACE

Black, frost-cold distance, sparsely honeycombed
　　With hollow shells of glimmering golden light;
　　Mere amber bubbles floating through the night,
Lit by one centred sparkle, azure-domed,
With circling motes where life hath lodged and
　　roamed.

ONE TOUCH OF NATURE

CRUEL and wild the battle:
Great horses plunged and reared,
And through dust-cloud and smoke-cloud,
Blood-red with sunset's angry flush,
You heard the gun-shots rattle,
And, 'mid hoof-tramp and rush,
The shrieks of women speared.

For it was Russ and Turcoman, —
No quarter asked or given;
A whirl of frenzied hate and death
Across the desert driven.
Look! the half-naked horde gives way,
Fleeing frantic without breath,
Or hope, or will; and on behind
The troopers storm, in blood-thirst blind,
While, like a dreadful fountain-play,
The swords flash up, and fall, and slay —
Wives, grandsires, baby brows and gray,
Groan after groan, yell upon yell —
Are men but fiends, and is earth hell?

Nay, for out of the flight and fear
Spurs a Russian cuirassier;

In his arms a child he bears.
Her little foot bleeds; stern she stares
Back at the ruin of her race.
The small hurt creature sheds no tear,
Nor utters cry; but clinging still
To this one arm that does not kill,
She stares back with her baby face.

Apart, fenced round with ruined gear,
The hurrying horseman finds a space,
Where, with face crouched upon her knee,
A woman cowers. You see him stoop
And reach the child down tenderly,
Then dash away to join his troop.

How came one pulse of pity there —
One heart that would not slay, but save —
In all that Christ-forgotten sight?
Was there, far north by Neva's wave,
Some Russian girl in sleep-robes white,
Making her peaceful evening prayer,
That Heaven's great mercy 'neath its care
Would keep and cover him to-night?

THE COUP DE GRACE

If I were very sure
That all was over betwixt you and me —
   That, while this endless absence I endure
With but one mood, one dream, one misery
Of waiting, you were happier to be free, —

   Then I might find again
In cloud and stream and all the winds that blow,
   Yea, even in the faces of my fellow-men,
The old companionship; and I might know
Once more the pulse of action, ere I go.

   But now I cannot rest,
While this one pleading, querulous tone without
   Breaks in and mars the music in my breast.
I open the closed door — lo! all about,
What seem your lingering footprints; then I doubt.

   Waken me from this sleep!
Strike fearless, let the naked truth-edge gleam!
   For while the beautiful old past I keep,
I am a phantom, and all mortals seem
But phantoms, and my life fades as a dream.

APPRECIATED

" Ah, could I but be understood ! "
   (I prayed the powers above),
" Could but some spirit, bright and good,
   Know me, and, knowing, love ! "

One summer's day there came to pass —
   A maid ; and it befell
She spied and knew me : yea, alas !
   She knew me all too well.

Gray were the eyes of Rosamund,
   And I could see them see
Through and through me, and beyond,
   And care no more for me.

ROLAND

A FOOLISH creature full of fears,
   He trembled for his fate,
And stood aghast to feel the earth
   Swing round her dizzy freight.

With timid foot he touched each plan,
   Sure that each plan would fail;
Behemoth's tread was his, it seemed,
   And every bridge too frail.

No glory of the night or day
   Lit any crown for him,
The tranquil past but breathed a mist
   To make the future dim.

The world, his birthright, seemed a cell,
   An iron heritage;
Man, a trapped creature, left to die
   Forgotten in his cage.

In every dark he held his breath
   And warded off a blow;
While at his shoulder still he sought
   Some tagging ghost of woe.

Spying the thorns but not the flowers,
　　Through all the blossoming land
He hugged his careful heart and shunned
　　The path on either hand.

The buds that broke their hearts to give
　　New odors to the air
He saw not; but he caught the scent
　　Of dead leaves everywhere.

Till on a day he came to know
　　He had not made the world;
That if he slept, as when he ran,
　　Each onward planet whirled.

He knew not where the vision fell,
　　Only all things grew plain —
As if some thatch broke through and let
　　A sunbeam cross his brain.

In beauty flushed the morning light,
　　With blessing dropped the rain,
All creatures were to him most fair,
　　Nor anything in vain.

He breathed the space that links the stars,
　　He rested on God's arm —
A man unmoved by accident,
　　Untouched by any harm.

The weary doubt if all is good,
The doubt if all is ill,
He left to Him who leaves to us
To know that all is well.

CLOUD TRACERY

WHAT wind from what celestial wood hath sown
Such delicate seed as springs in air, and turns
The blue heaven-garden to a bed of ferns
In feathery cloud ? They are not tossed, or blown

To such wild shapes, but motionless they ride,
Like a celestial frost-work on the pane
Of our sky-window, where the breath has lain
Of the pure cold upon the thither side.

They are but pencil touches, soft and light,
Traced faintly under some magnetic spell
By an entrancèd spirit, that would write

Hints of heaven-language ere the soul's release, —
Dim outlines of the syllables that tell
Of words like faith, and confidence, and peace.

THE LIFE NATURAL

OVERHEAD the leaf-song, on the upland slope;
Over that the azure, clean from base to cope;
Belle the mare beside me, drowsy from her lope.

Goldy-green the wheat-field, like a fluted wall
In the pleasant wind, with waves that rise and fall,
"Moving all together," if it "move at all."

Shakespeare in my pocket, lest I feel alone,
Lest the brooding landscape take a sombre tone;
Good to have a poet to fall back upon!

But the vivid beauty makes the book absurd:
What beside the real world is the written word?
Keep the page till winter, when no thrush is heard!

Why read Hamlet here? — what's Hecuba to me?
Let me read the grain-field; let me read the tree;
Let me read mine own heart, deep as I can see.

TO THE UNKNOWN SOUL

O SOUL, that somewhere art my very kin,
  From dusk and silence unto thee I call!
I know not where thou dwellest: if within
  A palace or a hut; if great or small
Thy state and store of fortune; if thou 'rt sad
This moment, or most glad;
  The lordliest monarch or the lowest thrall.

But well I know — since thou 'rt my counterpart —
  Thou bear'st a clouded spirit; full of doubt
And old misgiving, heaviness of heart
  And loneliness of mind; long wearied out
With climbing stairs that lead to nothing sure,
With chasing lights that lure,
  In the thick murk that wraps us all about.

As across many instruments a flute
  Breathes low, and only thrills its selfsame tone,
That wakes in music while the rest are mute,
  So send thy voice to me! Then I alone
Shall hear and answer; and we two will fare
Together, and each bear
  Twin burdens, lighter now than either one.

REPROOF IN LOVE

Because we are shut out from light,
  Each of the other's look and smile ;
Because the arms' and lips' delight
  Are past and dead, a weary while ;

Because the dawn, that joy has brought,
  Brings now but certainty of pain,
Nothing for you and me has bought
  The right to live our lives in vain.

Take not away the only lure
  That leads me on my lonely way,
To know you noble, sweet, and pure,
  Great in least service, day by day.

EVEN THERE

A TROOP of babes in Summer Land,
    At heaven's gate — the children's gate :
One lifts the latch with rosy hand,
    Then turns and, dimpling, asks her mate, —

" What was the last thing that you saw ? "
    " I lay and watched the dawn begin,
And suddenly, through the thatch of straw,
    A great, clear morning star laughed in."

" And you ? " " A floating thistle-down,
    Against June sky and cloud-wings white."
" And you ? " " A falling blow, a frown —
    It frights me yet ; oh, clasp me tight ! "

" And you ? " " A face through tears that smiled " —
    The trembling lips could speak no more ;
The blue eyes swam ; the lonely child
    Was homesick even at heaven's door.

ON SECOND THOUGHT

THE end's so near,
 It is all one
What track I steer,
 What work's begun.
 It is all one
 If *nothing*'s done,
The end's so near!

The end's so near,
 It is all one
What track thou steer,
 What work's begun —
 Some deed, *some* plan,
 As thou 'rt a man!
The end's so near!

INDEXES

INDEX OF FIRST LINES

INDEX OF TITLES

The Riverside Press
CAMBRIDGE . MASSACHUSETTS
U · S · A